PSYCHOLOGY
GONE AWRY

Books by the Author:

Mental Health: A Christian Approach
(coauthor)
Psychology Gone Awry
The Essence of Human Nature

PSYCHOLOGY GONE AWRY

An Analysis of Psychological World Views

MARK P. COSGROVE

ZONDERVAN
PUBLISHING HOUSE   OF THE ZONDERVAN CORPORATION
GRAND RAPIDS, MICHIGAN 49506

PSYCHOLOGY GONE AWRY:
AN ANALYSIS OF PSYCHOLOGICAL WORLD VIEWS

COPYRIGHT © 1979 by The Zondervan Corporation
Grand Rapids, Michigan

Library of Congress Cataloging in Publication Data

Cosgrove, Mark P
    Psychology gone awry.

    (A CEP book)
    1. Psychology—Philosophy. 2. Christianity—Philosophy. I. Title.
BF38.C754   150'.1   79-18503
ISBN 0-310-39101-6

Printed in the United States of America

1 **PSYCHOLOGICAL WORLD VIEWS** / 8

2 **THE HISTORICAL ROOTS OF MODERN PSYCHOLOGY** / 20

3 **NATURALISTIC PSYCHOLOGY** / 36

4 **MATERIALISM IN THE LABORATORY** / 52

5 **HUMANISTIC PSYCHOLOGY** / 70

6 **A HUMANISTIC SAND CASTLE** / 80

7 **TRANSPERSONAL PSYCHOLOGY** / 92

8 **TRANSPERSONAL EXPERIENCE AND TRUTH** / 110

9 **INADEQUATE PSYCHOLOGICAL WORLD VIEWS** / 126

10 **CHRISTIAN THEISM AND PSYCHOLOGY** / 136

NOTES / 150

INDEX / 158

It is difficult to fully understand psychology or any other academic field without first knowing its major assumptions about reality. We too readily yield to the idea that every scientist proceeds in an academically unbiased fashion, searching for truth wherever it may lie. This is certainly not the case. Psychology is practiced amid certain beliefs about the nature of reality and the nature of human beings. These beliefs shape the research goals, methods, and interpretations of the psychologist.

WORLD VIEW: A FILTER ON YOUR MIND

Such a fundamental belief structure is called a world view. It is a set of presuppositions (or beliefs) about the nature of the universe in which we live and our place within it. A world view may also be called a paradigm, or a set of control beliefs. It answers basic questions such as, What is the nature of a human being? Can I trust my senses? What is the origin of the universe and of human beings? Does the whole universe follow laws of cause and effect? Is there a god, and are there spirits? What happens when I die?

The answers to questions such as these and how strongly they are believed will affect the work of the psychologist. For example, psychologist John Doe believes that spirits may exist in the universe, whereas fellow psychologist Jane Smith does not. One Saturday they both read a newspaper account about an old man who claims his house is haunted.

How will each psychologist react to the story? Smith is more likely than Doe to believe the old man's report is fraudulent or the result of an overactive imagination. She is also less likely than Doe to investigate the haunting, to apply for a government grant to study such phenomena, or even to read a book about haunting spirits. If there were a whole culture of scientists like Smith, their books on psychology would probably not include a related topic such as demon possession except as a curiosity. In this example the efforts and findings of psychologists are affected by their world views.

Our assumptions about ghosts and haunted houses are not central to the development of a psychology of human beings, but underlying psychology there are major beliefs that have a profound effect on the entire nature of the discipline and its answers to key questions. Our world view affects what areas we feel are important enough to investigate, what methods we use in our study, how we interpret the facts we discover, and whether we are able to "see" certain types of solutions to anomalous data.

This book will deal with the assumptions surrounding today's psychological study of man. The study of psychology does not take place from the standpoint of just one world view but actually from at least three complete world views. These three psychological world views represent major ways of thinking about man and his problems. Each view is having a tremendous effect on the development of psychological theory and method, as well as on data interpretation.

The first of these three psychological world views is naturalistic psychology, which is composed of behaviorism and brain research. Those holding this view see persons as biological machines. The second world view is humanistic psychology; in this view a strong emphasis is placed on the human qualities of persons and the development of their self-potential. The third world view is that of transpersonal psychology. This view in psychology is concerned with the study of altered consciousness through medita-

PSYCHOLOGICAL WORLD VIEWS

tion, hallucinogenic drugs, and other related methods. These three world views are currently shaping psychological thought about the nature of persons, what experiments we are willing to do, what problems are to be solved, and how these problems are to be solved.

Someone might argue that we should attempt to work at our study of persons independently of any world view. That is, we should just gather data and let the facts speak for themselves. Actually, many psychologists claim to be doing exactly that. But the point remains that no one can proceed to make scientific statements without holding basic assumptions in certain areas. Often psychologists are not aware of their hidden assumptions and how they affect their work. Most scientific psychology begins with the assumptions that the universe is real; that it operates by dependable, discoverable laws; and that I can trust my basic observations. Even these beliefs are a part of a world view.

We must also realize that world views, like theories and models, which are more limited belief structures than world views, can be helpful to science and experimental discovery. World views stimulate our thought in certain directions. They put boundaries around our wild speculations. We need a world view to do our best psychology. It is important, though, to be aware of the assumptions in our world view and why we hold them. Assumptions can be logically held and carefully compared to the data collected in the real world. They can be rejected or modified if logic and data clearly demand it.

When we investigate the three world views of psychology, we will see that each view has its limitations. Each is an attempt to explain only part of the data collected in psychological laboratories. If a world view is true, it must fit all the facts we are able to gather. Another problem is that one belief in a psychologist's world view is often incompatible with another belief in the same world view. Such conflict is not permissible. If a world view is to be regarded as true and valid, it must be logically consistent within itself.

There is in psychology a need for a comprehensive, consistent world view by which the excellent research that has been done can be tied together. Unlike the physical and natural sciences, in which fair agreement has been found for the interpretation of data, psychology is in a state of flux, because psychologists hold wide and varying opinions about the nature of humanity and of human problems. This book will conclude with a suggestion for a more complete world view for psychology than has been set forth, one that takes into account the best of the three current world views. This world view is Christian theism, in which human beings are seen as created, crippled by sin, and designed for spiritual life. It will be suggested that it is this view alone that best fits the data on human beings.

Another value of world-view thinking is that it helps student learning. It has been my experience in teaching that learning proceeds faster and is more satisfying when one understands the framework within which the data must fit. A close look at psychological world views is an opportunity to really understand psychology and the nature of persons. If psychology has gone awry, it is because it does not have a satisfactory world view.

In addition, our world-view investigation is important, and not just an academic exercise, because the findings and applications of psychology greatly affect our everyday lives. The types of counselors we go to with our problems, the fads being dangled before us, the bold new plans of psychoengineers—all are a result of psychology's world views.

THE MAJOR COMPONENTS
OF A PSYCHOLOGICAL WORLD VIEW

The four major components of a psychological world view are (1) the nature of reality, (2) the nature of human beings, (3) the nature of the problems of humanity, and (4) the nature of solutions to the problems of humanity. Most psychologists have presuppositions (consciously or unconsciously) in these four areas. We will see that it is their answers to questions about these areas that separate psychologists into naturalistic, humanistic, and transpersonal ways of seeing reality and man.

These three world views are ways of thinking and not schools of psychology. Therefore, it is not possible to pigeonhole every psychologist with one of these labels. Some psychologists have world views that are hybrid mixtures of these three.

Today's psychology is divided into broad areas of investigation, such as clinical, educational, experimental, industrial, and social. Psychologists have tried to stay away from establishing schools of thought. But world-view thinking takes place even in the most specific of laboratory investigations. For example, a scientist may study the effect of a rat's thirst level on its sexual behavior. However, even in such a specific study the research has arisen from a world view—probably the naturalistic world view. A psychologist with a different way of seeing reality might not have thought of using animals as subjects or of using behavior as data. Just because a person is not aware of or concerned with his world view does not mean that it is not there affecting his work.

The Nature of Reality

1. *Its composition.* One's view of all reality—the universe and our immediate world—is basic. What is reality made of? Matter? Nonmatter? Both? Is there more to the universe than I can perceive or understand, such as spirit beings or new dimensions?

2. *Order in the universe.* We can also ask questions about the nature of order in the universe. Does the nature of order follow laws of cause and effect in the universe? Depending upon how one answers the questions on the composition of the universe, one can also ask, Is there a *physical* cause for every effect in the universe? One who believes that the universe is a totally closed system, composed of physical matter alone, must believe that any effect we see, such as human mental activity, must have a physical cause.

3. *Knowledge of the universe.* Finally, we need to ask how we come to know things about the universe and its component parts. This area of thinking is known as epistemology to the philosopher. A person is a skeptic who denies that people really know what they ordinarily claim to know. Or if one believes that the universe operates by cause and effect, one might manipulate things to see effects, thereby gaining an understanding of the cause-effect sequence. This is the prime method of science. One could, however, believe that truth is learned by experiencing it more directly. When you taste a milk shake, you are learning things about it that a strict scientific method would never reveal.

Religious revelation (holy writings, dreams, etc.) and rationalism (philosophical logic) are also claimed by many to be methods of knowing. An individual may also hold to a magical view of the universe, in which things may happen for no scientific reason. Knowledge, then, comes by intuitive, non-rational methods.

The answers to all three of these questions—the composition of the universe, order in the universe, and knowledge of the universe—may seem very obvious to the reader, but it is not so to everyone. A set of answers seems obvious to you because you have been schooled in one way of thinking, and it is difficult to see things any other way. Some people believe the universe as we see it is not real, but only an illusion. If someone on the street asked you to prove to him that this whole universe is not just a part of some big dream, how would you do that? He is obviously coming from a different world view. You might push his foot under a passing truck to convince him of the reality of physical objects, but that would not be very nice! We cannot really "prove" our world view to him, but we can logically talk to him about our assumptions, why we hold them, and their implications.

The Nature of Human Beings

Our second category of questions, concerning our own nature, is very important in psychology. Note, however, that answers in this category depend in some ways on the answers to the previous questions about the nature of the universe. This is because humankind is a part of the universe we observe.

1. *The essence of human beings.* Are people made only of matter, or are they more? In other words, do they have immaterial minds or souls? If a person holds that the universe contains no immaterial substance or personalities, it is difficult to claim that people have immaterial minds or souls. The answers to these questions are important because one's concept of the essence of people has to be sufficient to explain all that they think, feel, and do. We must

explain their loving, crying, blushing, self-reflecting, going to the moon, or writing a poem.

2. *The will of human beings.* A question related to that of the essence of human beings concerns their will. Is their behavior determined or free? Again the previous presuppositions affect the answer to this question. If the universe is composed of only matter and people are made of only matter, then their behavior is determined.

3. *The origin of human beings.* Another difficult question concerns the origin of humans. We would like to explain the origin of all that we see in human nature. If you believe that a person is more than just matter, the explanation of origins becomes more complicated. How does a mind or a soul arise from matter? Obviously, evolutionary theory is one of the suggested answers, but it has many difficulties for the psychologist who assumes man has a mind.

4. *The purpose of human beings.* We can also ask about the purpose and destiny of humans. Do people live just to eat and die, or is there something more? We must ask this question in human psychology, while we might not do so in the study of animal biology, because of the high aspirations and goals people have and because of the obvious lack of fulfillment of their aspirations and goals. Is it unfulfilled purpose, a low consciousness level, or a blocked relationship with Deity that is the cause of this lack? And, lastly, we can ask whether people survive the grave, and if so, in what fashion.

The Nature of the Problems of Humanity

Nearly everyone will admit that humans are not in an optimum state of being. They have problems and frustrations. Civilizations rise and fall. Technology outstrips morality. The growth of crime outdoes population growth. Population outgrows food supply and human concern. What's wrong with people? They have more success and more failure than any other creature on the globe. Everyone has a name for what is wrong: emotional behavior, tragic flaw, cultural lag, or irrational thinking.

Assumptions in this area deal with the cause of people's problems. Is the cause bad environment, lack of education, incomplete evolution, or a sinful nature? Are people cut off from their true potential, or do they just not have the potential to live successfully? Are they beasts evolving upward or angels fallen down?

We could wait for the scientific data to be collected and hopefully answer these questions. However, remember that, depending on our assumptions about the nature of the universe and people, we are already putting boundaries on our explanations for human beings' problems. If people are made only of matter, their problems have to be material. If the universe is multidimensional, however, maybe people need to transcend a merely material dimension of experience and enter into another dimension. If they have minds, perhaps the problems lie there. If people have spirits, they could have spiritual problems.

The Nature of Solutions
to the Problems of Humanity

Of course, what we assume about solutions to people's problems is almost completely fixed by our previous assumptions. How we define the composition of the universe determines the possible make-up of human nature, and thus the possible sources of human problems. Mental therapies, for example, vary with one's world view. Psychology's world views vary greatly; therefore, therapies range from brain surgery to deep meditation. As psychiatrist James Mallory and I pointed out in a previous book, psychologists' psychotherapies depend on their view of people and their problems and the goals they have for their clients as persons.[1] Changes in society also depend on how one views the individual person and his needs.

We must also make certain assumptions about the morality of our solutions to people's problems. The ethics of experimentation and implementation does not come from science, but from one's view of human nature. The value that we place on persons within the universe and society influences our decisions about what is "moral" in relationship to them.

CONCLUSION

The major questions we should resolve as we continue in this book are questions of world view. Therefore, for each world view analyzed we will ask, Just what is this world view? Is it consistent within itself? Does it fit the best data we find in psychology?

How psychology developed to where it is today, divided into these three major world views, is the subject of our next chapter. Ideas don't just happen. They flow. And the thought patterns and presuppositions of psychology today are not so much the result of laboratory investigation as they are the result of ideas in the past.

In the beginning were Wisdom and Confusion. And they begat Humanism, who lived one thousand years, begetting sons and daughters. Humanism begat Empiricism, who married Evolution, and they begat Old Psychology. Old Psychology lived only thirty years and begat three children: Behaviorism, who married Brain Research, both of whom were very neat and proper; Humanistic Psychology, a kindly child named after its grandfather; and Transpersonal Psychology, who was a very odd child indeed.

Mark Cosgrove

THE HISTORICAL ROOTS OF MODERN PSYCHOLOGY

The major assumptions of modern psychology are not so much the result of laboratory research as they are inheritances from systems of thought before the founding of psychology as an organized discipline. It is traditionally said that psychology as an academic field was "born" in the laboratory of Wilhelm Wundt in Leipzig, Germany, in 1879. The world view that was current in academic circles at that time had a tremendous effect on the new science of human behavior. Why that world view was popular and how it affected psychology will be traced in this chapter. Let us look at a series of ideas through history that have affected the development of modern psychological world views.

PRESCIENTIFIC THOUGHT ON HUMAN NATURE

Whenever we hear the word *prescientific*, we immediately think of primitive thought. By no means is this correct. Early thought on human behavior was skilled and insightful and in many ways more complete than current thinking. We may excel in our description of the biology of humans, but we do not excel in the description of the psychology of their inner nature.

Plato and Aristotle clarified the already ancient belief that reality was derived from two substances, or principles. These two substances were the material (rocks, animals, brains, etc.) and the immaterial (God, spirit, mind, soul). This split in reality has been referred to as dualism.

Plato placed an emphasis on the immaterial mind of man and his ability to think and reason. Aristotle, a biologist as well as a philosopher, had the opposite emphasis: he believed that the need for systematic, objective observation was a basis for knowledge about man. Of course, man was a unique creature in both of these dualistic views because he participated in both forms of reality; he was a part of both worlds. He was obviously physical, and yet just as obviously mental, as a thinker. It was maintained in this early, dualistic view that man had a soul or mind inside the body and that at death the soul was freed. This dualistic thinking can lead to the tendency to see the physical part of man as evil, the source of uncontrollable drives and desires at war with the mind. The Christian church picked up this thinking along with Greek dualism, and in the church's early history she stressed the importance of the spiritual nature of man at the expense of the physical. Later, in the 1200s, the theologian-philosopher Thomas Aquinas attempted to provide more of a balance in the study of man as he tried to reconcile the writings of Aristotle with the theology of the church.

RENAISSANCE HUMANISM: THE AGE OF MAN

The emphasis on the spiritual nature of man in this dualistic mode of thinking continued for the first thousand years after Christ. The study of human nature was largely confined to the soul, and the theologian was the investigator. However, a later blossoming of thought called humanism had a tremendous effect on the study of human nature. Humanism was a system of thought flowering in the 1200s–1600s and continuing to the present. It emphasized the glories of reason and the greatness and self-sufficiency of man.

The humanists felt that the church had overemphasized God, the legions of saints, the sin nature, and the terrible bodily and worldly sins. It was during this period of human confidence that people took an interest in themselves, their abilities, and their physical natures. Paintings depicted human subject matter that emphasized the physical element of dualism. The beautiful realism of Michelangelo and Raphael bears witness to this. People explored the globe and in general had an optimistic outlook about their potential and worth as they emerged from the Dark Ages. Spanish coins before the time of Columbus bore the inscription *Ne Plus Ultra*, meaning, "There Is Nothing Beyond" (Spain and the Pillars of Hercules). After his time the *Ne* was removed. There *was* "more beyond." This age began with the Renaissance in art (1200s) and continued with the phenomenal rise of science (1600s), the latter having a major effect on the study of man.

THE BIRTH OF SCIENCE

The renewed interest in man and the world and the confidence in the ability of humans, using their reasoning powers, to investigate their own natures and the world helped in the phenomenal rise of science in the 1600s. A particular world view developed in which it was said that the physical world behaved according to fixed laws and that these laws were discoverable by reason; this world view helped people to investigate nature.

One authority attributes the rise of science to two great beliefs: "The belief in a logically and aesthetically perfect 'natural order' from which the laws of nature can be deduced, and the determination to put every theory to an empirical test. . . ."[1] This world view was dominated by Christian thought, in which it was taught that the creation was the product of an orderly God and that the abilities of man's mind, though fallen, were His gift.[2] This Christian base was soon to change, however. The immaterial dimension of dualism—which included the super-natural, the human soul, the immaterial human mind, and values and morals from outside of man—was to receive less emphasis due to the development of a new, scientific world view. Two forces helped shape this world view: Cartesian dualism and empiricism.

CARTESIAN DUALISM

One notable person of this period was René Descartes (1596–1650). He was distinguished in many fields, from mathematics and physiology to philosophy. He suggested a solution to the difficulty of applying the new scientific methodologies to the immaterial part of man, which seemed to be beyond scientific testing. This solution came to be known as Cartesian dualism. He said that the world was a duality composed of extended substance (body) and thinking substance (mind). He felt that some intellectual processes could actually proceed without the intercession of the soul. This confirmed emphasis on dualism virtually guaranteed that the scientist could be free to study only the body of man. The difficult study of the mind, or the soul, could be left to the philosophers and theologians.

Another type of dualism from a German, Gottfried Leibniz, widened the split between mind and body even more. Leibniz disagreed with the idea of interaction between body and mind stressed by Descartes. Leibniz taught that the body follows its own laws and is mechanical. Mental acts must be explained in terms of mental causes. The soul acts without any direct reaction on the body. This type of dualism is known as parallelism. Mind and body, according to Leibniz, seem to interact only because of a preestablished harmony between them.

The Historical Roots of Modern Psychology

24

On the contrary, this type of dualism can actually hinder one from making accurate explanations of human nature. First, it is possible that man may be better examined as a unity. While it is difficult to study man as a unity, to do so may actually be more accurate scientifically and theologically than to examine him with dualistic presuppositions. An inaccurate picture of the brain may be obtained without considering the mind, or vice versa. During the making of electrical probes of brain areas, mind processes will still accompany the resultant brain activity. Second, one of the problems of holding to dualism was that it allowed the methods of study of those who wished to adhere to the world view of materialistic monism, i.e., that observable matter was all there was to man, to prevail. This resulted in the first major influence on the soon-to-be-founded field of psychology—empiricism. Also, by the 1800s theologians were themselves abandoning confidence in spiritual reality in their "new theology." The study of the soul and spirit deteriorated in the face of biblical criticism and the rise of evolutionary theory.

EMPIRICISM

Empiricism is the name of a way of thinking that is at the core of modern science. Empiricists believe that knowledge comes through the medium of the senses, i.e., physical things that we can see, hear, etc. This of course eliminates any investigation of the mind of man because mind cannot be so studied. The "mind," according to empiricist John Locke, is a tabula rasa, a blank slate on which sensory experience is written.

Even more radically, many empiricists presuppose that whatever cannot be shown to register as sensory information, such as mind or spirit, doesn't exist. That is a remarkable assumption. But note that it is only an assumption, a belief. One cannot prove the mind doesn't exist by scientific methods when he admits that his tools are insensitive to measuring immaterial things, if they do exist.

Empirical thinking represents the shifting of a world view. Before empirical thinking became predominant, reality was dualistic—material and immaterial. Humans could have souls or minds. After empiricism took over, reality was considered to be composed of only matter, including the nature of man. I can learn only what the empirical method of science will say about man. What does this do to the study of concepts such as God, ghosts, or mind? At best, it limits the investigation of them; at worst, it eliminates them from consideration as real phenomena. In empiricism the study of that creature called man, who seemed by experience to partake of both material and immaterial spheres of reality, is to be only a biological study. Only part of him is studied, or even admitted to exist.

All this was taking place before psychology, the field in which the human mind and human behavior are studied, got its start. The nature of human nature was already being decided before the experiments began in the psychological laboratory.

This empirical way of thinking we will call the first root in the psychology family tree. There is nothing wrong with science and empiricism, but not being aware of the limits of the empirical method in the study of reality can lead to erroneous conclusions in the study of the human personality. In other words, one can use the empirical method but he must not be limited by it. The empirical or scientific method must be supplemented by methods not strictly scientific—such as those of history, theology,

THE HISTORICAL ROOTS OF MODERN PSYCHOLOGY

and philosophy—to help us discern man's inner nature.

THE THEORY OF EVOLUTION

A result of empirical thinking and the second great root in the formation of psychological thinking was evolutionary theory:

> The influence of Darwinism upon psychology during the last quarter of the nineteenth century did as much as any single factor to shape science as it exists today.[3]

When psychology finally arrived on the scientific scene, psychologists thought the way they did about human nature primarily because of the philosophical roots of psychology in the then-current materialistic, empirical world view and not because of the psychological data collected.

The job of empirical scientists was to explain what they saw in nature. The earth supports a variety of nonliving things and living things, both simple and complex. People are self-conscious and intelligent. They seem to be at the peak of nature. How did they become all that they are? The materialistic, empirical world view demanded a naturalistic explanation (as opposed to a supernatural one like creation). The way of thinking of the time was ripe for a naturalistic theory like evolution.

Those who espoused evolution as a theory proposed that the characteristics we see in humans are the result of millions of years of gradual change from simple organisms to more complex ones. Human nature is the end result of those changes. The process of change is by natural selection, by which those organisms survived that were best adapted to their environment and its requirements for living. After millions of years the most fit creatures developed. The human being is the pinnacle of such an evolutionary spiral. The theory was also expanded to include the formation of the first life from the lifeless chemicals of the planet, as well as the chemicals themselves from random combinations of molecules.

Darwin (1809–1882) first formalized the theory of evolution of animals, including humans, in the famous *Origin of Species* [4] in 1859, just twenty years before the birth date of psychology. In his *Descent of Man* (1871) [5] he discussed the human being in the evolutionary tree. Evolution as an idea was certainly prompted by Darwin's observation of the similarities among animals, but the current, naturalistic world view advocates, who were looking for an explanation for the complexity of humans and human nature, saw in evolution an answer to their questions. How could a material world produce a human being? In other words, Darwin was seeing animal and fossil similarities through the glasses of naturalism, and evolution was the result. How mind could evolve from biological processes was not a central issue, since the mind was being lost sight of in empiricism.

Once evolution was accepted as a valid scientific view, it allowed the developing field of psychology to use animal subjects in experimentation and to make generalizations about human nature from these conclusions. It is not surprising, then, that claims are made that psychological research supports evolution. W. Lambert Gardiner in a popular introductory psychology text said, "Most of us feel better about being raised apes than fallen angels. Darwin's theory of evolution has provided one of the basic axioms in modern man's conception of himself." [6] The animal nature of humans has not been discovered by psychologists; it has been assumed by their chosen world view. For example, psychologists today investigate the human brain with very little dependence on human subjects (and understandably so, since it is very difficult to get them to volunteer for experimentation). Animal brains are similar to those of humans, but when we start making declarations about the nature of human cognition, it may not be the data that are speaking so loudly, declaring that humans are only animals. We will look into some of these data in chapter 4, where we deal with naturalistic psychology.

THE BIRTH OF PSYCHOLOGY

We have finally arrived at the birth of psychology, the study of human nature. But first let us review. The dualistic world view was gradually reduced to materialistic monism. The older view, that reality (including humans) was composed of both matter and mind, gave way to a new, empirical, naturalistic view of reality—that it was composed of matter alone. Humanism sparked interest in the natural world and created confidence in the mind of man to investigate that world. The believers in empiricism, the child of humanistic confidence, limited the world to the material by assuming it to be so. Evolution, a part of this materialistic way of thinking, was a theory to explain man in terms of the physical.

It was in 1879 that Wilhelm Wundt (1832–1920), the father of psychology, started the first psychological laboratory in Leipzig, Germany. Actually, psychological investigations began some years earlier with E. H. Weber, Gustav Fechner, Johannes Müller, and Hermann von Helmholtz. Isn't it predictable that the men involved in the development of psychology had their prime interests in physics, chemistry, and physiology? That was to be expected since in the current world view man was limited to the material, and by then the physical sciences were well developed.

Wundt's laboratory was called a laboratory of psychophysics because through psychology he was going to relate the mind (*psyche*) and conscious experience to biology and matter (*physike*). Wundt's book *Principles of Physiological Psychology* (1873–74) was an investigation of psychology by physiological methods. At this time psychologists still admitted the existence of conscious experience (it is hard to deny one's own), but felt it must have its basis in matter itself. In introspection, the chosen method of psychophysicists, sensory experience was to be broken down into its smallest mental elements. This was copied from the methods of chemistry, by which all things were seen to be composed of combinations of basic elements. So too, the rich, personal experience of a human must be composed of combinations of smaller elements of experience. In the experimental method of introspection, a subject would, for example, look at a picture and report that he experienced a certain color and a certain level of brightness. The prime question to Wundt was, What are the basic, irreducible sensations that make up the structure of the subject's conscious experience? For this reason Wundt's school of psychology was called structuralism. Such thinking made it easier for later psychologists to identify basic conscious experience with the activity of brain cells. The many firings of different neurons equals the conscious person.

THE RISE OF BEHAVIORISM

The method of introspection did not long remain the method used by psychologists because it did not completely fit the empirical method of science. Psychologists were studying the mind and analyzing reported experiences that were unverifiable by the scientific method. The empiricist says, "You said you saw a blue light. I don't know if you did or even what you truly experienced. How can I properly study an individual's private experience?" Introspection was also inadequate for the study of children, the insane, and animals, since they could not reliably report experience, if at all.

Consider this problem. How does one study the phenomenon of love? In psychological terminology, love is an emotion, or feeling. If you were Wundt, you could catalog hundreds of "basic" feelings and, after much effort, suggest a combination of such feelings that might make up the experience of being in love. This research would be tedious and even impossible to complete in any satisfactory manner. However, the main objection of the empiricist is that such a method of research is dealing with data that cannot be seen or properly measured. The psychologist is still asking the subject what he feels. The report gives valid scientific data: "Subject 6 reported he was in love." But how do we know what subject 6 means by "love"? Is there not something better than a subjective report of an inner experience?

An American psychologist, John Watson (1878–1958), the father of behaviorism, said that to study psychology scientifically one must study that which he or she can best see and measure. Watson said:

> In 1912 the behaviorists reached the conclusion that they could no longer be content to work with intangibles and unapproachables. They decided either to give up psychology or to make it a natural science. . . . The behaviorist asks: Why don't we make what we can observe the real field of psychology? . . . Now what can we observe? Well, we can observe behavior—what the organism does or says.[7]

Vague reports in imprecise language about mental states are useless to an empiricist. But one can see and quantitatively measure the behavior of people, their actions, or their physiological responses that accompany reported experiences. Instead of studying love feelings (whatever they are), let us, says the behaviorist, study dating behavior, or sexual behavior, or helping behavior.

The behaviorists also developed operational definitions of their subject of study. These were definitions in terms of quantity or number. Love might be operationally defined as fifteen dates with the same person. Love correlates well enough with dating so that it can be stated that people in love often date regularly, but are we accurate in reducing an inner feeling of love to a number of dates? Many frequent daters would disagree. Obviously something is lost in the quest to be empirical.

THE REBELLIONS: HUMANISTIC AND TRANSPERSONAL

Behaviorism, with its strongly naturalistic explanations about human nature, left people with a personal dissatisfaction. People believe they are more than muscle and brain, more than chimp, but science seems to say they are not.

Many of the post-Freudians, such as Harry Stack Sullivan, Erich Fromm, and Karen Horney, refused to limit humans to being nature's machines, and they stressed conscious thought and the social nature of man. There are also cognitive psychologists, such as child psychologist Jean Piaget, who emphasize the activity of the mind of the person and innate elements of mental activity, as opposed to the concept of the mind as a blank slate.

It wasn't until the early 1950s, however, that a full-fledged rebellion took place in psychology that gained ground lost to behaviorism. Humanistic psychology was the name of a movement started by psychologists Abraham Maslow, Carl Rogers, and others. The humanistic psychologists rejected the behaviorists' view that man is a mere behaving machine and the psychoanalytic view that personality is ruled by unconscious forces. The humanistic psychologists wanted a full-fledged study of the whole person: body, behavior, and the even more important aspects of thinking, feeling, loving, and living.

The teachings of humanistic psychology brought a return to a view of man as being composed of more than merely the physical; man is also mind and all that is essential to being human. The proponents of humanistic psychology emphasized two things: (1) the basic goodness, worth, and potential of man and (2) his internal experiences and humanity (not just animal qualities). These psychologists did not reject science, but they refused to be limited by it in the study of people.

As we will later discover, most humanistic psychologists did not reject naturalistic assumptions such as the philosophical theory of materialism concerning the universe and evolution. Therefore, the humanistic psychologist faced some unanswered questions. How did man get mental life from an unthinking universe? Why is man so worthwhile and to be valued?

These are hard questions to answer for the humanistic psychologist. One way out of this world-view problem would have been for him to cut the naturalistic ties that bound him and to become less attached to the naturalistic world view. Humanistic psychologists were not about to return to the long road of theistic dualism, however, and another non-naturalistic system—Eastern psychology—appeared just in time to gain their following. This last way, taken by some humanistic psychologists, leads to the transpersonal rebellion.

TRANSPERSONAL PSYCHOLOGY

At first transpersonal psychology was just a "back room" version of humanistic psychology, and many still consider it just that. Recently, however, it has become a full-fledged movement. Abraham Maslow himself spearheaded this school in the late 1960s. Transpersonal psychology deals with the "spiritual" nature of man and is involved with the study of diverse topics such as extrasensory perception, drug experiences, biofeedback, meditation, and Eastern religions. The term *transpersonal* refers to the move to transcend man's present, personal experience to some ultimate experience. This thinking is a long way from empiricism. Not only was mind sneaking back into psychology, but also experiences beyond the mind.

Transpersonal thinking began earlier than the 1960s and Abraham Maslow. In fact, William James and Carl Jung were psychology's earliest transpersonal thinkers. James gave his views on these topics in his *Varieties of Religious Experience* (1902),[8] and Jung discussed transpersonal phenomena in his "Synchronicity: An Acausal Connecting Principle" (1955).[9] This new movement in psychology recognizes that man has a mind and a spiritual nature. The nonphysical world exists, and we need to be conscious on its level. This movement has been popular because its supporters can admit the existence of mental and spiritual components of man's nature by changing the limited, naturalistic world view. However, the world view that transpersonal psychology begins to embrace is one very similar to that of many

THE HISTORICAL ROOTS OF MODERN PSYCHOLOGY

Eastern religions. There is no doubt that this shifting thought pattern is changing modern psychology.

CONCLUSION

So then, in psychology today there are three major world views competing for our attention. Behaviorism and brain research are the strongest, being direct products of a naturalistic world view that pervades our academic culture. Their proponents fill our university chairs and fund the grants for research. The humanistic psychologists, who strike out against the abuses of naturalistic thinking, have gained much ground. Transpersonal psychology, the most recent force, has in its romance with the East and with paranormal phenomena, gained a broad, "newsstand" popularity and has enough scientific credibility to enter the academic arena as well.

In the next six chapters we will examine each of these psychological world views and the uses and abuses of the thinking of their advocates. We will look carefully at the data in psychology to see which of the world views finds the most support. We will be looking at each world view to consider what it lacks as an adequate world view. With the limitations of each in mind, I will suggest a more adequate world view for the psychological sciences. This will be one that fits the entire range of data in psychology and does more justice to both science and the spiritual nature of man than do any of the other world views.

Naturalistic psychology represents mainstream psychology. It is embraced by many psychologists who have behavioristic and neurophysiological interests. These psychologists include some experimental and cognitive psychologists who are well integrated into the behavioral and physiological mainstream of thought. The term *naturalistic* is taken from the philosophy of naturalism in which a physical or natural explanation for all that happens is sought. Naturalistic psychologists hold to materialism (all is matter) and empiricism (knowledge through sensory experience). Behavior as conditioned by environment and behavior reduced to the machinery of the brain are the objects of study of naturalistic psychologists, who have had a profound influence on our thinking about man. Let us now construct the world view of the naturalistic psychologist. While doing this, we need to remember that not every behaviorist or brain physiologist has this complete world view, but the following does represent the mainstream consensus of thought brought to bear on the field of psychology by these psychologists.

THE MAJOR COMPONENTS
OF THE NATURALISTIC WORLD VIEW

The Nature of Reality

1. *The universe.* While most psychologists do not spend time discussing the nature of the universe, their apparent viewpoint is that the combination of matter and energy comprise the "stuff" of the universe. Complicated arrangements of atoms make up all that we "see." This viewpoint excludes the existence of nonphysical or spiritual substance or beings.

According to this viewpoint the complexity and organization that we see in matter (stars, animals, etc.) result from matter + energy + time + chance.

All things evolved from disorder to order and complexity. The origin of the universe was a "big bang" from a primal block of matter (Big Bang Theory) or a continuous creation of hydrogen atoms from nowhere and from nothing (Steady State Theory). While there are serious, logical problems with believing in a universe composed of only matter and with believing in its origin from nothing, most psychologists are not trained or interested enough in fields such as physics and astronomy to be even aware of the problems.

2. *Knowledge.* The prevalent view of naturalistic psychologists as to how we know (epistemology) follows from the naturalistic, materialistic view of the universe. The universe is seen as being orderly and regular, following cause-and-effect rules. Therefore, all knowledge can be perceived through the application of the scientific method so that effects are manipulated in order that causes may be discerned.

Empiricism is the rule for the naturalistic psychologist. Because of empiricism (the basic assumption of science), the naturalistic psychologist says that we can know only what is transmitted through our senses. Empiricism can be called knowledge by sensory experience. The naturalistic psychologist is not concerned with studying the soul or ghosts, none of which can be sensed directly. If a person sees a ghost, it must be a dream or a delusion. Since the empiricist believes that all effects have natural causes, when he analyzes mental experiences, ghosts, or miracle claims, he looks for natural, material causes.

The Nature of Man

1. *Man is only material.* Note that by the time a psychologist starts to presuppose about the human

condition, he is limited by the boundaries set up in his assumption about the nature of reality. If the assumption of materialism is true concerning the nature of reality, there are few options left to him to believe about the nature of man. If the universe is composed only of matter, and if we assume man to be a part of the universe, every part of man is made only of matter. However, if a person has a demonstrable, immaterial essence, the materialist must explain its origin from matter. Some psychologists take the former route (that every part of a human is composed only of matter), while others, who believe the mind exists, hold that it is a direct product of brain function (epiphenomenalism).

This assumption that the human is made of nothing but biological processes leads to what is known as reductionism. Reductionism means that everything about persons (mental aspects, social mores, etc.) is explainable in terms of matter, usually by means of biology and chemistry. Look at these statements from two naturalistic scientists. The belief that man is only a construction of matter is clear in this statement by Robert Doty:

> Nor can all the rulings of the Church or law ever hope to define at what instant within the womb the spinning threads of deoxyribonucleic acid have from mere chemicals produced an immortal, supernatural being.[1]

Behaviorist B. F. Skinner also outlines his beliefs in his book *Beyond Freedom and Dignity:*

> But what about man himself? Is there not something about a person which is more than a living body? Unless something called a self survives, how can we speak of self-knowledge or self-control? To whom is the injunction "know thyself" addressed?[2]

Skinner then answers his own question:

> The picture which emerges from a scientific analysis is not a body with a person inside, but of a body which *is* a person in the sense that it displays a complex repertoire of behavior.[3]

Thinkers like Skinner reduce the whole, conscious person to his biological and chemical parts. For example, a brain physiologist would look at the human experience of hunger and decide that it was totally the result of the brain activity at that moment. Or he would say that the motivation for success is the combination of certain hormones, body tensions, and memories locked within the physical body. This thinking is very empirical and operational. Thought itself is reduced to the electrochemical activity of billions of neurons in the brain. Certainly the brain is involved in hunger, love, and thought, but the question is, Is the material activity of the brain sufficient to explain all involved in human nature? We will see evidence in chapter 4 that it is not. But today many scholars think it is very scientific to reduce the human mind to observable, countable, physiological events.

2. *Man is determined.* According to a pure empiricist, since matter operates by cause-and-effect rules, and thus is determined, and since man is only matter, he must be determined in his behavior. That is, there is a physical cause for every thought or action that we see in him. Man is assumed to be a biological machine. There are many types of determinism, some of which allow for a certain amount of human freedom. There is no doubt that man is material in part, and hence materialistic rules will explain some of his actions. But if man has an immaterial mind, it is possible that the free mind is one of the causes of his behavior. If one denies the immaterial mind,

however, there is no room for free will. Even the belief in an epiphenomenal mind (a mind directly a product of brain states) will not provide for freedom of thought, since mind in that case is totally dependent on brain activity.

The famous expositor of the determined individual is B. F. Skinner. Skinner's brand of naturalistic psychology is behaviorism. He feels that biology and brain control all human action and that the controller of the brain is the environment. The environment reinforces responses with physiologically satisfying stimuli. To Skinner, these environmental reinforcers are the determiners of man's behavior. He speaks thus about man:

> Autonomous man is a device used to explain what we cannot explain in any other way. He has been constructed from our ignorance, and as our understanding increases, the very stuff of which he is composed vanishes. Science does not dehumanize man, it dehomunculizes him, and it must do so if it is to prevent the abolition of the human species. To man qua man we readily say good riddance. Only by dispossessing him can we turn to the real causes of human behavior. Only then can we turn from the miraculous to the natural, from the inaccessible to the manipulable. . . .
>
> Man is a machine in the sense that he is a complex system behaving in lawful ways, but the complexity is extraordinary. . . .
>
> A scientific analysis of behavior dispossesses autonomous man and turns the control he has been said to exert over to the environment.[4]

3. *The human is an animal.* Evolution is the generally held theory as to the formation of the human species. In *The Naked Ape* Desmond Morris stated:

> I am a zoologist and the naked ape is an animal. He is therefore fair game for my pen and I refuse to avoid him any longer simply because some of his behavior patterns are rather complex and impressive. My excuse is that, in be-

coming so erudite, *Homo Sapiens* has remained a naked ape nevertheless; in acquiring lofty new motives, he has lost none of the earthly old ones. This is frequently a cause of some embarrassment to him, but his old impulses have been with him for millions of years, his new ones only a few thousand at the most—and there is not hope of quickly shrugging off the accumulated genetic legacy of his whole evolutionary past. He would be a far less worried and more fulfilled animal if only he would face up to this fact.[5]

Eugene Linden, in his book *Apes, Men, and Language*, praises the removal of the Platonic model of man by which distinctions between humans and animals were emphasized, in favor of an evolutionary one:

> Darwin has provided the basis for a paradigm that might explain both human psychology and human behavior in terms of man's continuity with the rest of nature rather than his discontinuity.[6]

We see the same evolutionary ideas presented in the new field of sociobiology, which is a synthesis of the principles of evolutionary biology and of the social sciences. This field, which is growing in influence, was begun by Edward Wilson with his mammoth volume *Sociobiology: The New Synthesis*. David Barash, of the departments of biology and psychology at the University of Washington and author of *Sociobiology and Behavior*, says:

> I propose that evolutionary theory may also contribute a valuable paradigm for all of the life sciences and especially for the study of animal behavior, both human and nonhuman.[7]

Notice that Barash wants to apply a world view to interpret social science data.

The Nature of Man's Problems

Given the assumptions of materialism and determinism, naturalistic psychologists are limited in defining the ultimate nature of man's problems. If we assume that materialism, determinism, and evolution are correct views, the source of man's personal and social problems must be rooted in the material. We have two candidates for the material source of human problems: physiological causes and environmental causes.

1. *Physiological causes.* Those who hold the position that physiological causes are at the base of problems such as crime, depression, hatred, alcoholism, schizophrenia, etc., structure our thinking in the direction of brain pathology as a cure for the problems. The naturalist must seek out and develop such material explanations.

Even though factors other than brain mechanics are involved in producing negative, human emotions and behavior, there is a major, scientific thrust attempting to demonstrate that physical manipulation of the brain alone can produce these emotional and motivational states in man.

From the laboratory of José Delgado there are reports that electrical stimulation of the brain will reliably evoke a true rage in both cats and monkeys. The same results are claimed for human subjects. Delgado writes, "In one of our female patients, stimulation of a similar area in the thalamus induced a typically fearful expression, and she turned to either side, visually exploring the room behind her."[8] Interpretations such as this leave the impression that when a brain area was activated the activation alone produced, or equaled, the emotional state of the woman. We will discuss a different interpretation of such data in the next chapter.

Remember our discussion of world views. Someone who wears naturalistic "glasses" will tend to conclude that brain stimulation alone causes human emotions. One could, however, be wearing world-view "glasses" that take into account cognition and thus more easily think of cognitive factors that may, in combination with brain stimulation, produce the emotion felt. Cognitive factors such as the patient's fear of doctors and her uneasiness at having electricity applied to her brain then would accompany and affect physiological changes.

Some scientists feel that the human problem is that of incomplete evolution. Nobel prize–winner Konrad Lorenz, who wrote *On Aggression*, believes that man evolved aggressive instincts but has lagged behind in the evolution of restraints on aggression. [9]

One recent theorist says that there is an inherited genetic structure that produces selfish desires. This theory is proposed in the recent book *The Selfish Gene* by zoologist Richard Dawkins. He says:

> The argument of this book is that we, and all other animals, are machines created by our genes. Like successful Chicago gangsters, our genes have survived, in some cases for millions of years, in a highly competitive world. This entitles us to expect certain qualities in our genes. I shall argue that a predominant quality to be expected in a successful gene is ruthless selfishness. [10]

The question to consider, though, is one of world view. Is man composed of merely matter? If he is more than matter, his problems are more than merely material in nature. Let us not deny that people do consist of matter, that they have material problems, and that these interact with nearly every mental problem they can have; however, does the *brain's* part in human experience justify the claim that human problems are rooted in biology? The naturalistic world view, not the data, answers yes. Looking past psychological influences to physiological ones is the result of the materialistic presupposition of these scientists. It is more likely that the brain and heredity are involved in human problems as merely influences and predispositions toward a particular mental state than that the brain and heredity are the causes of these problems.

2. *Environmental causes.* To the naturalistic psychologist the explanation for human problems may be one of poor environmental conditioning. In the law of operant conditioning it is said that behavior followed by a suitable reinforcement is likely to be repeated. Therefore, a rat that accidentally depresses a lever in its random movements in a cage will tend to press the lever again if the action is immediately reinforced with food by the experimenter. Pressing the lever does not have to be and usually is not a conscious thought on the part of the animal, i.e., "I will get food if I press the lever." The rat just behaves that way, and the behavior can be described in terms of predictable laws. Therefore, if a man is a criminal, says the naturalistic psychologist, it is because he grew up in a ghetto or a bad home and was reinforced for bad behavior.

B. F. Skinner has contrasted thinking in terms of mind and emotions versus behavior and environment in regard to human problems. Skinner obviously favors the behavioristic explanation for problems (which he puts in parentheses and italics below):

> Consider a young man whose world has suddenly changed. He has graduated from college and is going to work, let us say, or has been inducted into the armed services. Most of the behavior he has acquired up to this point proves useless in his new environment. The behavior he actually exhibits can be described, and the description translated, as follows: he lacks assurance or feels insecure or is unsure of himself (his behavior is weak and inappropriate); he is dissatisfied

or discouraged (he is seldom reinforced, and as a result his behavior undergoes extinction); he is frustrated (extinction is accompanied by emotional responses); he feels uneasy or anxious (his behavior frequently has unavoidable aversive consequences which have emotional effects); there is nothing he wants to do or enjoys doing well, he has no feeling of craftmanship, no sense of leading a purposeful life, no sense of accomplishment (he is rarely reinforced for doing anything); he feels guilty or ashamed (he has previously been punished for idleness or failure, which now evokes emotional responses); he is disappointed in himself or disgusted with himself (he is no longer reinforced by the admiration of others, and the extinction which follows has emotional effects). . . .

What he tells us about his feelings may permit us to make some informed guesses about what is wrong with the contingencies, but we must go directly to the contingencies if we want to be sure, *and it is the contingencies which must be changed if his behavior is to be changed.*[11]

By contingencies Skinner means the contingencies of reinforcement in the environment.

Let us not be caught denying environmental *influences*. We ought to study to find out how much of an influence the environment is on human behavior, without limiting ourselves to the equation of heredity + environment = behavior. The ones with the naturalistic world view do write this equation. Those with other world views can believe in the thinking, deciding person. It is assumption, not data, that eliminates the person and gives us the biological machine.

The Nature of Solutions

By the time we get to the proposed solutions of the naturalistic psychologist to personal and social problems, you can guess the type of solutions they would be. Problems are material (physiological or environmental), and thus solutions have to be in those two areas to be effective. Therefore, it is meaningless for a naturalistic psychologist to talk about mental or spiritual approaches to solving human problems. Let us examine these two areas of naturalistic solutions.

1. *Change physiology.* There are many examples of the physiological approach to solving human problems. One example is the effort to treat mental diseases with measures such as psychosurgery, which is the removal or destruction of brain areas. This is not practiced much today, but from 1936 to the mid-1950s some fifty thousand such operations were performed. Such surgery has fallen into disuse because of the widespread use of tranquilizers. The side effects of psychosurgery may include the loss of mental and emotional functions.

The point to make here is that the initial idea to operate on the brain for mental problems and the decision to continue such operations in spite of negative side effects have come from a world view in which it is maintained that a *person equals brain activity.* In his book *Brain Control* brain researcher Elliot Valenstein agrees:

> It is not surprising that the belief in the anatomical bases of mental illness encouraged people to explore the possibility that some surgical intervention might produce beneficial effects. [12]

Today it is more frequently electroshock therapy (EST) or drug therapies that are used by the naturalistic therapist to control human, emotional problems than some form of psychosurgery. EST is the passing of a fairly strong, but brief, electrical current directly through the brain. The patient loses consciousness immediately (thus feeling no pain) and goes into convulsions for about a minute. EST does relieve many disorderly emotional symptoms and, in conjunction with other types of psychotherapy, can be an effective treatment.

In the mid-1950s the beginning of widespread use of drug therapy to combat emotional disturbances was begun. The three major classes of drugs in this field are tranquilizers used to calm agitated persons, energizers used to improve the mood of the depressed, and antipsychotics used to control hallucinations and other symptoms of psychosis.

Though these techniques are more effective and appropriate than psychosurgery, the idea is still to search for physical solutions to *mental* problems. The naturalistic psychologist needs to ask himself if a solely material solution is the right path to solving mental problems or if he or she is just slavishly attached to a particular world view and thus cannot see or appreciate other approaches.

Currently, much publicity is being given to the new techniques of bioengineering, by which genetic make-up might be altered to produce better, problem-free human beings. Robert Sinsheimer, biologist at California Institute of Technology, says that it is time to take evolution into our own hands through genetic and physiological manipulation and to usher in a new human being:

> However near the time may be at which we will start doing it, I think this possibility of making deliberate genetic changes in man is potentially one of the most important concepts to arise in the history of his race. I can think of none with greater long-range implications for the future of our species. Indeed, this whole concept marks a turning point in the whole evolution of life. Even in the ancient myths man was constrained by his essence. He could not rise above his nature to chart his destiny. This day we can envision that chance and choice.[13]

NATURALISTIC PSYCHOLOGY

A feel for the naturalistic hopes can be gained by reading popular books such as *Future Shock, Brave New World, A Clockwork Orange,* or *The Second Genesis.* [14] All suggest that man's deepest problems can be solved on the biological level.

2. *Change environment.* Of course, the behaviorist agrees with the physiologist about biological problems in man's nature, but he cannot see that these problems are always brain pathology. To him it is more often environmental pathology that is causing the problems. Human problems arise from reinforcement for unacceptable behavior patterns in society. The techniques of behavior modification are proposed for the classroom, the hospital, and society at large. The psychologists using behavior modification feel that insight into, or understanding of, one's problems is unnecessary. Instead, they seek to change or remove troublesome behavior. A typical classroom situation could involve students being reinforced for reading with playtime out-of-doors. The mental patient who itches constantly is reinforced during periods of nonitching. The delinquent boy collects little blue tokens for good behavior that can then be used for buying candy at the store or for gaining more free time at the library.

The whole modification process depends on finding an adequate reinforcer for the person and on providing expert guidance with gradual, shaping techniques toward some desired behavior. The process is unconscious, and people are supposed to really feel as if they want to do what they are being reinforced to do.

These principles can be applied to individuals or to designing an entire culture. Such applied behaviorism is described in Skinner's interesting, utopian novel, *Walden II,* in which a whole community of healthy, happy people is developed by such operant techniques.[15]

At the close of his *Beyond Freedom and Dignity,* Skinner suggests that this applied behaviorism is not just fiction:

> Physical and biological technologies have alleviated pestilence and famine and many painful, dangerous, and exhausting features of daily life, and behavioral technology can begin to alleviate other kinds of ills. In the analysis of human behavior it is just possible that we are slightly beyond Newton's position in the analysis of light, for we are beginning to make technological applications. There are wonderful possibilities—and all the more wonderful because traditional approaches have been so ineffective. It is hard to imagine a world in which people live together without quarreling, maintain themselves by producing the food, shelter, and clothing they need, enjoy themselves and contribute to the enjoyment of others in art, music, literature, and games, consume only a reasonable part of the resources of the world and add as little as possible to its pollution, bear no more children than can be raised decently, continue to explore the world around them and discover better ways of dealing with it, and come to know themselves accurately and, therefore, manage themselves effectively. Yet all this is possible.[16]

It is easy to see that Skinner believes that behavioral technology is the answer to every human problem.

THE POSITIVE CONTRIBUTIONS OF NATURALISTIC PSYCHOLOGY

Before leaving this chapter, some of the positive points of naturalistic psychology should be stated.

1. There are many accurate statements in its world view. It is true that man has a body. We should believe that the material can always be a part of man's problems and, hence, the solution to problems. Since it is likely that man does have a mind closely associated with the brain, even naturalistic

brain research can tell us much about the mind and human nature.

2. Man is determined and unconscious in some of his behavior, and many individuals are partially controlled by reinforcement. The psychologist should never forget this as an influence on human behavior.

3. We can learn much from those similarities that animals have to humans, no matter what the reason for the similarities.

Let us end this chapter with a question. Can you limit man to the material and knowledge about man to the empirical and still be studying him in his entirety? The next chapter will discuss evidences that show why psychology needs more than just a naturalistic view of human nature.

4

Because of the mystery of our being as unique self-conscious existences, we can have hope as we set our own soft sensitive and fleeting personal experience against the terror and immensity of illimitable space and time. Are we not participants in the meaning where there is else no meaning? Do we not experience and delight in fellowship, joy, harmony, truth, love and beauty where there else is only the mindless universe?

Sir John Eccles

MATERIALISM IN THE LABORATORY

Once we enter the laboratory, we will see that the major assumptions of naturalistic psychology (materialism, determinism, and personality evolution) are tenuous at best. It is not my purpose in this chapter to carry out a complete evaluation of naturalistic psychology. I have begun that in another book in which I deal with these questions: Is man merely material? Is man determined? Is man animal?[1] Such an investigation is important in every field of academic endeavor. We must be willing to compare our world-view assumptions with the real world of data.

What I would like to do here is to look at some physiological data on the mind-brain question and to demonstrate how the naturalistic psychologist's assumption of materialism can bend the interpretation of data to favor his view. This is not the result of dishonesty or of tampering with the data but of assuming the very things in one's method that he wishes to prove.

Materialism is the belief that all that exists in the universe, including man, is in its entirety composed of matter and energy. This excludes the existence of immaterial beings or of concepts like soul or mind. This assumption leads the naturalistic psychologist to say that all he observes about another person—his thinking, acting, and feeling—is a direct product of physical brain activity alone. In carrying out his investigations, he is empirical ("I can know only what enters into me through my senses") and a behaviorist (behavior is the only subject matter of psychology). These conclusions lead him to gather only behavioristic data and to reject subjective reports of human experience (phenomenological data) as unscientific. This restriction on the data to be collected leads the psychologist to the false conclusion that brain activity equals all that a person is. Perhaps it can be shown that brain activity equals one's behavior. However, brain activity alone does not equal the total person when we look at him or her as a being of inner experience as well as of outer behavior. If we admit phenomenological data in physiological experimentation, it is necessary to postulate an immaterial mind to explain all the data, because the brain alone is an insufficient cause to explain all the data.

In summary, we will look at several types of experiments in order to show how the materialist at best shows only that changes in the brain are correlated with changes in behavior. If one collects only behavioral data, of course, he will find that brain equals person. However, if he allows the "unpardonable sin" of subjective reports to be considered during brain experiments, he will find that the subject's personality is more than brain activity alone.

I am not in any way arguing that the brain does not influence people and that it does not play a major role in all that a person is mentally. I am only suggesting that the brain alone is not sufficient to explain all mental phenomena. Let us examine three types of data in support of this thesis.

NEURON FIRING AND EXPERIENCE

There is nothing about the material of neurons that would lead anyone to predict that their electrical-chemical activity would produce experience. Neurons, or nerve cells, are the individualized components of which the whole brain is built. Approximately ten billion neurons are densely packed into the human brain. The major purpose of neural activity is to pass messages throughout the body in the form of increased electrical-chemical activity. Each neuron is able to discharge stored, electrical energy in short bursts like a car battery does at a rate of several times per second to one thousand times per second. Each burst is called a neuron "firing." This firing activity is passed from one neuron to another over a tiny space called a synapse, or synaptic cleft, by means of chemical activity.

The firing is obviously a signal that is correlated with the outside world of stimulation. A light of increasing brightness causes visual-system neurons to increase their firing rate. Neurons in the auditory system increase their firing to sound frequency and then engage in more complicated coding for frequencies above these neurons' top speeds. In such ways the outside world becomes represented in neuron firing patterns.

If we are willing to examine subject reports and not just to study the human subject as a biological machine, we must answer the question, Why do we *experience* the world when it becomes represented in neuron firing? Neurons fire, and we *see* sights and *hear* sounds. When does the firing of a neuron turn into an experience? Why can two, apparently identical neurons, firing at the same rate, produce two separate experiences? A visual-system neuron may fire at the same rate as an auditory-system neuron, and yet one may *see* blue in one case and *hear* an eight-thousand-cycle-per-second tone in another. The neurons are passing their signals to different areas in the brain cortex (place theory), but this is labeling, not explaining, the phenomena. There is a need for something beyond the material brain to turn signal into experience. Of course, this does not mean that we know *how that happens*, only *that it does happen.*

Brain activity explanations are not sufficient to

explain experience. We cannot even perfectly corre-late neuron firing with experience. Many times, for example, neuron firing continues when experience stops, as when one is asleep. At that time one's expe-rience is greatly reduced, or even eliminated. The same phenomenon is observed in the waking state when we consider the concept of attention. It is not the firing of neurons per se that produces experience but it is one's awareness of, or the turning of one's mind toward, that input stimulation. Certainly the brain reduces the firing of neurons or blocks their transmission through the brain stem to higher brain areas, but the point remains that we are experienc-ing only a fractional part of the neural activity in our brains at any one moment. Therefore, we cannot equate neural firing per se with our experience. This fact makes it very difficult for the materialist to deny the force of human, subjective experience and thus to deny that something more than a brain-produced (epiphenomenal) mind exists. An epiphenomenal mind, according to its definition, is a direct product of brain states and thus should correlate as perfectly as we can measure with brain activity. The epiphenomenal mind, however, is not the mind we observe in the laboratory. It is only by denying the validity of phenomenological data or by not using them that anyone can say that brain experiments prove the immaterial mind does not exist.

BRAIN ACTIVITY
AND COMPLICATED BEHAVIOR

The brain can be activated, or made to fire, by an experimenter's direct intervention. The use of wire electrodes to stimulate the brain electrically, or of micropipettes to stimulate it chemically, allows experimenters to manufacture brain activity. The prediction of the naturalistic scientist is then, "I can manufacture all the person is when I manufacture appropriate brain states, since the person is the brain in operation." When the empirical, behavioristic experimenter limits observation of a person during experimentation to his or her behavior, the experimenter is indeed assuming what he has set out to test, i.e., if one stimulates the brain, a set of behaviors (the whole person) results.

We read about hundreds of experiments in which the brain of a monkey is stimulated and the monkey then engages in some behavior such as blinking an eye. Twenty thousand times an electrical current is applied, and, like a light bulb, the monkey is "turned on." It blinks its eye twenty thousand times, never growing weary of this behavior. The same type of experiment is done with human subjects. On an operating table and with local anesthesia, the brain of a person who is awake is stimulated, causing the person to move his finger or his whole arm. The prediction then is seemingly verified, i.e., that brain activity equals behavior (the whole person).

Even complicated behaviors can result from such experiments. José Delgado in his book *Physical Control of the Mind* reports that brain stimulation has reliably set in motion the required neural activity needed to induce walking—with apparently normal characteristics:

> Monkey Ludy had one contact planted in the red nucleus, and when it was stimulated for 5 seconds, the following effects appeared. . . . (1) immediate interruption of spontaneous activity; (2) change in facial expression; (3) turning of the head to the right; (4) standing on two feet; (5) circling to the right; (6) walking on two feet with perfect balance, using both arms to maintain equilibrium during bipedestation; (7) climbing a pole; (8) descending to the floor; (9) uttering a growl; (10) threatening and often at-

tacking and biting a subordinate monkey; (11) changing aggressive attitude and approaching the rest of the group in a friendly manner; (12) resuming peaceful spontaneous behavior. This complex sequence of events took place during ten to fourteen seconds always in the same order. . . .[2]

If this were all the data available to us—behavioral data—it would appear that brain activity does equal a complicated person. But as soon as we are willing to look beyond behavior to subjective experience, we arrive at a different interpretation of the experiments. This interpretation does not equate the person with his brain activity alone but rather only equates some of his behavior with his brain.

It should be noted that repeated brain stimulation does not reliably produce identical behaviors. Elliot Valenstein, author of *Brain Control,* agrees that reliable behavior production is not the norm in brain stimulation studies:

> The impression exists that if electrodes are placed in a specific part of the brain, a particular behavior can inevitably be evoked. Those who have participated in this research know that this is definitely not the case.[3]

Mental awareness can play a part in the behavior of animal subjects, and certainly in that of human subjects. Delgado speaks of an interesting observation of monkey Ludy: "Ludy avoided obstacles in her path, walked with excellent coordination, and used normal strategies in her fights."[4] If we placed a six-hundred-pound bear in her path, there is no doubt that though the electrical stimulation would continue, her awareness of the bear would drastically affect behavior.

It is most enlightening to ask a human subject what he or she is experiencing during brain stimulation. If a human brain is stimulated so that the patient raises his arm or finger, the person's report always includes a mental awareness that is different from the brain state produced. Neurophysiologist Wilder Penfield stated that "when a subject observes such an action, he remarks, 'That is due to something done to me and is not done by me.'"[5] Sir John Eccles says concerning a similar experiment with human subjects, in response to materialist C. Wade Savage:

> Ask the subjects of the experiment, who are well-trained neuroscientists. I have myself discussed the experiment with all of them whom I have met on many occasions. They are unanimous in stating that they experience it as a mental act at the time of the voluntary movements of their finger. . . . In fact, the very essence of the design of the experiment was that it had to be a free act initiated without any reference to any signal or to any imposed timing. Later we are told by Dr. Savage that "the cause of my finger flexion is my neural activity, it is mental activity in me, and in that sense it is *I* who move my finger." This is just the old obscurantist materialism which refuses to recognize the experience of willing because it conflicts with dogmatic belief.[6]

Jose Delgado reports this example:

> In one of our patients, stimulation of the left parietal cortex through implanted electrodes evoked a flexion of the right hand starting with contraction of the first two fingers and continuing with flexion of the other fingers. The closed fist was then maintained for the rest of the 5-second stimulation. This effect was not unpleasant or disturbing, and it developed without interrupting ongoing behavior or spontaneous conversation. The patient was aware that his hand had moved involuntarily but he was not afraid and only under questioning did he comment that his arm felt "weak and dizzy." When the patient was warned of the oncoming stimulation and was asked to try to keep his fingers extended, he could not prevent the evoked movement and commented, "I guess, Doctor, that your electricity is

stronger than my will." If this stimulation was applied while the subject was voluntarily using his hand, for instance to turn the pages of a magazine, this action was not blocked but the induced hand flexion distorted voluntary performance and resulted in crumpling and tearing of pages. In our experience and in reports by other investigators, electrical stimulation of the motor cortex has not induced precise or skillful movments, and in all cases the evoked responses have been clumsy and abnormal.[7]

It is more than clear that the subject's brain state and resulting behavior should not be equated with the whole person, as his own experiences reveal. If any phenomenological data is ignored or minimized, misleading interpretations about the brain and the mind will result. These misleading interpretations are compounded when there is no attempt made in physiological experiments to control mental processes of subjects during electrode stimulation. Of course, if an experimenter does not believe in the existence of the mind, he will not attempt to control it as he manipulates brain states. This is important to consider because brain stimulation seems to produce only vague, generalized states of arousal in human subjects, and not complex behaviors, feelings, or ideas. Complex, well-defined behaviors, feelings, and ideas following brain stimulation could, as an alternative way of thinking, be due to a mind state that adds richness and definition to vague feelings of arousal.

One good example of this thought concerns electrode stimulation and sexual arousal in a female patient who had psychomotor epilepsy that could not be controlled by medication:

Electrodes were implanted in her right temporal lobe and upon stimulation of a contact located in the superior part about thirty millimeters below the surface, the patient re-

MATERIALISM IN THE LABORATORY

ported a pleasant tingling sensation in the left side of her body "from my face down to the bottom of my legs." She started giggling and making funny comments, stating that she enjoyed the sensation "very much." Repetition of these stimulations made the patient more communicative and flirtatious, and she ended by openly expressing her desire to marry the therapist.[8]

It is important not to interpret this experiment as the strict materialist would by saying that the electrode created a brain state that created her amorous behavior. Unless mind states such as her thoughts about her male therapist and about her previous amorous experiences were controlled, it is more reasonable to assume that her mind states had the major influence in shaping her behavior. How do we know what her behavior would have been if the therapist had looked like the hunchback of Notre Dame? Even Delgado admits the effect of personality on behavior:

In the interpretation of these results it is necessary to consider the psychological context in which electrical stimulation occurs, because the personality configuration of the subject, including both current psychodynamic and psychogenetic aspects, may be an essential determinant of the results of stimulation.[9]

Only a phenomenologically minded experimenter would try several therapists, including a woman therapist, to record the different behaviors of a patient under electrical stimulation. The experimenter could also analyze several patients of varying amorous backgrounds. Only an experimenter who admits the possibility of the existence of the mind feels the need to do the kind of studies that would reveal the actions of a mind. Therefore, world view does shape the data we publish. We definitely need more phenomenologically oriented scientists involved in brain research.

THE SPLIT BRAIN:
TWO BEHAVIORS, ONE MIND

Other areas of concern are the split-brain preparation and its effects and how these effects are interpreted by the materialistically minded psychologist. To split the brain is a legitimate, medical procedure used to control severe epilepsy. The human brain is composed of two large hemispheres connected by a body of cells called the corpus callosum. In a person afflicted with severe epilepsy, the corpus callosum tends to involve the entire brain in seizure activity, even if the disturbance is initially limited to one side. Cutting the corpus callosum and splitting the brain hemispheres reduces the effects of epileptic seizures.

The split-brain person is otherwise unaffected by the operation because both halves of the brain have the same experiences at the same time. Under specialized testing, however (first made by Roger Sperry and his associates at the California Institute of Technology), differences in cerebral function were observed. The left, and dominant, hemisphere governs the use of language, mathematical computation, and orderly and analytical tasks. The right hemisphere seems superior at handling holistic, global, or relational tasks such as art, music, and the recognition of faces.

The importance of split-brain studies for our discussion here is that experimenters were enabled by the separating of the two hemispheres to demonstrate that each hemisphere could perform independently of the other and engage in different, even competing, tasks simultaneously.

MATERIALISM IN THE LABORATORY

For example, a dollar sign can be flashed to the right side of the brain and a question mark to the left side. If the person is asked to draw with his left hand (which is controlled by the right side of the brain) what he sees, he will draw the dollar sign. Remember that his right brain has no speech center. If he is then asked what he has drawn (using his speaking half, which is directed from the left side of the brain), he will say that he drew a question mark. In short, one hemisphere does not know what is happening in the other. Monkeys with split brains have even been taught to perform two separate, conflicting tasks, each carried out by a separate hand-eye-brain unit.

How the data from these studies are interpreted depends on one's world view. It should be pointed out at the outset that Sperry himself does not see these studies as evidence of absolute materialism in the human mind, but many materialists do use them as such. The prediction of the materialist is this: if the human mind and personality equal the brain in action, then if we divide the brain, we will have two minds in one body. The materialistically inclined experimenter then analyzes a split-brain person. Being completely empirical and not wishing to collect a report from the subject about his experience, he observes the subject's behavior. What does he find? He discovers that the subject exhibits two different behavior patterns. Therefore, his conclusion is that there must be two different persons in the head after a split-brain operation.

Here is an interpretation of the split-brain experiment in a popular, introductory psychology text.

> Split brain research is interesting and informative in its own right. But, more importantly, it seems (to this author, at any rate) to resolve many of the questions about what the "mind" is or where it is to be found. If dividing the brain produces

two separate "minds" or spheres of consciousness, then it follows that consciousness is nothing more or less than the electrical and chemical activity of the brain. In humans, the terms "mind," "brain activity," and "consciousness" are simply different ways of describing the same set of events.[10]

Neil Carlson, author of a physiological psychology textbook, shares the same view:

> The point of this discussion is that the mind is the result of a functioning brain. The fact that disconnecting the hemispheres gives rise to two distinct minds—with different capacities, memories, and (probably) personalities—provides, I believe, the most persuasive proof that the unity of our conscious awareness is a product of the interconnections of the various regions of the brain.[11]

The mistake that each of the above authors is making is in their defining consciousness as behavior. Since the person is doing two different things, he must have two separate conscious experiences, they maintain. Unfortunately, the right hemisphere is silent and cannot communicate, and the only consciousness from which we get a report is the left hemisphere. If we are willing to ask the subject, we get his report of a unity of experience. At the extreme we must be agnostic as to whether or not there is another person in the right hemisphere. Behavioral data alone misleads one into saying there are two "persons" in the split brain.

It is important as well to draw a distinction between consciousness and self-consciousness. The right brain-eye-hand unit does many things that suggest it is independently conscious. The right hemisphere can perceive and react to its own sensory input in a similar way as the left hemisphere. However, even if consciousness is in some way the product of neural activity, not consciousness but self-consciousness must be equated with our experience of being persons. The left hemisphere is not only conscious, but self-conscious as well. If the resultant behavior shown by the right hemisphere leads one to expect that it is conscious, this behavior is not the type that would indicate self-consciousness. Therefore, it is possible to propose there is a separate consciousness (from that in the left hemisphere) in the right hemisphere, although unconscious activity is perhaps a better description of what occurs, since it is known how much unconscious, complicated activity can take place in humans and machines. Subjects themselves report on activity of the silent right hemisphere, not as if someone else were controlling their bodies (another person), but as if it were an unconscious activity of their own. (See the Eccles quote below.)

The error is with those who say there are two persons, one in each hemisphere, because even the behavioral data does not suggest self-consciousness for the right hemisphere. Nobel Prize–winner Sir John Eccles shares this latter interpretation of the split-brain data. We could say that Eccles is a dualist who believes that the dominant left hemisphere is the "seat of the soul" or the prime material through which the mind works. He says:

> Furthermore, Sperry's (1968, 1970a, 1970b) investigations on commissurotomy patients have shown that the dominant linguistic hemisphere is uniquely concerned in giving conscious experience to the subject and in mediating his willed actions. It is not denied that some other consciousness may be associated with the intelligent and learned behavior of the minor hemisphere, but the absence of linguistic or symbolic communication at an adequate level prevents this from being discovered. It is not therefore "self-consciousness." The situation is equivalent to the problem of animal consciousness, to which we should be agnostic. [12]

Sperry himself, on the basis of his famous split-brain experiments, also is not willing to say that the person equals his brain:

> Surgical separation of the hemispheres, especially the deeper bisections we perform in animals, I have interpreted as resulting in the creation of two distinct domains of consciousness. This says nothing about *self*-consciousness. It remains to be determined how much, if any, self-consciousness is present in the disconnected minor hemisphere of man.[13]

Make no mistake. Sperry is not a dualist. He believes in an emergent mind in which "mental phenomena are conceived to be determined by—and built from —neural events. . . ."[14] He is, however, telling us that split-brain data do not support the notion that two persons inhabit the split-brain's head.

Therefore, we can conclude this look at the split-brain studies and agree that a split-brain subject shows two separate and even competing behaviors. A split-brain subject *may* have two separate consciousnesses, although it seems preferable at this point in the research to speak of the right hemisphere as *unconscious, complex, and behavior-directing.* No, we cannot say there are two distinct, self-conscious persons in a split-brain's head. The split-brain studies have been overpublicized for the apparent reason that they seem to fit the materialistic assumptions underlying our modern biological and psychological sciences.

In summary, we can see how the world view of naturalistic psychologists can actually influence data collection in such a way that it seemingly supports the very ideas that were assumed by those psychologists all along. If one assumes that materialism—the belief that man and nature are made of only matter—is factual, he is likely to accept

MATERIALISM IN THE LABORATORY

empiricism as a basis for knowledge and behaviorism as his data base. Once he begins collecting behavioral data and says he is observing "person," he has lost his objectivity, and his world view is only feeding itself.

This is true of every other world view we will look at in psychology. The key is not to do away with world views in science but for one to be aware of his assumptions, to know why he holds them, and to recognize how they affect his approach to, and interpretation of, data in the real world.

For these reasons we must reject the naturalistic psychologist's world view as too rigid for a study of man and its materialistic assumptions as incompatible with the best data we collect on man. Though we have not taken the time to analyze data with regard to every segment of the naturalistic world view, it becomes obvious that if we reject its materialism, we must also reject determinism as regards humans. This is because determinism is an assumption that depends on the assumption of the materialism of man's being. This does not *prove* free will. I am only stating that one cannot assume that strict determinism is true for man. We must also hesitate before we so easily assume the evolution of the person and the mind of man. Putting the responsibility for the production of a self-conscious mind on the shoulders of a biological theory like evolution is extremely unwise. There is a great discontinuity between mind and brain, and matter and nonmatter; and we cannot easily assume that mind just emerged from matter suddenly and completely or that all matter has mind (panpsychism). Much evidence, in fact, supports the traditional, creation hypothesis, that a personal, immaterial, creative God is the source of mind and personality in man.

Since we have turned aside from the major assumptions of naturalistic psychology, let us now examine a world view that accepts both person and mind as part of man's essence.

5

By now in 1960, America has produced so . . .
much *cold, analytical, scientific psychology—scientific in the narrow-minded, brain-injured sense
of the term—we've seen so much of this gimmick
psychology that we've forgotten that it was man in
all his richness that we set out to know.*

Gene F. Nameche

HUMANISTIC
PSYCHOLOGY

Dissatisfaction with the naturalistic and psychoanalytic approaches to human personality led many psychologists to forge a new way of thinking about man. It was known as the *Third Force* in psychology—after behavioristic and psychoanalytic thought—or more popularly as humanistic psychology. Beginning in the early 1950s, this humanistic thinking represented a distillation of ideas from neo-Freudians, gestalt psychology, existential psychology, and phenomenology. Its leading proponents were persons such as Abraham Maslow, Carl Rogers, Gordon Allport, Erich Fromm, Victor Frankl, Rollo May, and Karen Horney among others.

In general, humanistic psychologists see man's healthy, conscious self as the subject matter of psychology. The data of concern in humanistic psychology consist of

those human capacities and potentialities that have little or no systematic place, either in positive or behaviorist theory or in classical psychoanalytic theory: e.g., love, creativity, self, growth, organism, basic need gratification, self actualization, higher values, being, becoming, spontaneity, play, humor, affection, naturalness, warmth, ego transcendence, objectivity, autonomy, responsibility, meaning, fair play, transcendental experience, psychological health, and related concepts.[1]

Human nature to the humanistic psychologist is seen as good and full of potential. Hence a great deal of attention is paid to solving human problems such as human motivation, life's goals, crime, and war, as opposed to classical perception or animal behavior concerns. Carl Rogers, for example, has often discussed psychology's relationship to social issues such as population, the cities, marriage, racism, education, and the Vietnam War.[2]

THE MAJOR COMPONENTS
OF HUMANISTIC PSYCHOLOGY

The Nature of Reality

1. *The universe.* There is little discussion in the camp of the humanistic psychologist concerning the nature of reality. In general, ours is a naturalistic academic culture, and the humanistic psychologist shares the academic views of those who do not resort to supernatural agency to explain all that exists. Therefore, all reality is seen as impersonal, mechanical, and evolved. There are conscious beings in the universe, namely, man and some higher animals, that are products of the evolving universe. The humanistic psychologist does not differ from the naturalistic psychologist in this assumption. We catch this materialistic foundation in the words of Carl Rogers:

> From the existential perspective, from within the phenomenological internal frame of reference, man does not simply have the characteristics of a machine, he is not simply a being in the grip of unconscious motives, he is a person who creates meaning in life, a person who embodies a dimension of subjective freedom. *He is a figure who, though he may be alone in a vastly complex universe, and though he may be part and parcel of that universe and its destiny,* is also able in his inner life to transcend the material universe.[3] (emphasis mine)

2. *The nature of knowledge.* Since humanistic psychologists believe in the cause-effect order of the universe, they believe that we can learn about the universe with the scientific method, but they are strongly convinced that science is limited in the study of man. This is true, say they, because only material quantity, and not the qualities of human experience, can be revealed through science. Therefore, instead of having a concern for the operational,

behavioral definitions of human experience, the humanistic psychologist goes straight to the experience itself as data. In contrast to empiricism or sensory experience, this method of knowing can be called human experience. This can be in the form of personal reports or even the accounts of experience in the great literature of the world. If all humans have the same basic needs, it follows that self-knowledge leads to an understanding of every individual in the entire human race. In this brand of psychology we can ask a person about his or her feelings and needs, believing it is better to investigate the whole person with a loose, experimental method than to investigate dull parts of a human with traditional, rigorous, scientific methods. Again I quote from Carl Rogers:

> Within myself—from within my own internal frame of reference—I may "know" that I love or hate, sense, perceive, comprehend. . . . Thus one important way of knowing is through the formation of inner hypotheses which are checked by referring to our inward flow of experiencing as we live in our subjective interaction with inner or outer events. This type of knowing is fundamental to everyday living. Note that though external cues and stimuli may be involved in this type of hypothesis formation, it is not the external situation against which we test our hypotheses. It is our inner experiencing to which we refer to check and sharpen and further differentiate the conceptual hypotheses we are forming from the implicit meanings.[4]

One observation is that humanistic psychologists begin to inject into psychology a relativism in knowledge at this point: "Humanistic psychology postulates a universe of infinite possibility. Thus it recognizes that all knowledge is relative and subject to change."[5] Since I am the object of study, that which I experience is being defined as truth, says the humanistic psychologist. We can see this phenomenon in group sessions, in which individuals take turns relating how they feel about a conflict. Nobody attempts to discover who is really at fault in the conflict since the important subject matter is how the group session participant feels about the conflict. What has happened is that the humanistic psychologist has redefined truth. It is no longer an objective reality for him. Experiences and feelings are the prime stuff of reality. It is this emphasis on experience that made it easier for the humanistic psychologist to move toward the experience epistemology of the transpersonal psychologies by the 1970s.

The Nature of Man

1. *Man has mind.* The humanistic psychologist recognizes that man has a body, a brain, and reactive processes, but he also recognizes that these are hardly the whole of human nature. Man has a mind and can think and feel. He is a person with hopes, dreams, fears, needs, and frustrations. J. F. T. Bugental, in his article "The Third Force in Psychology," said,

> A central fact of human experience is that man is aware. Awareness is postulated to be continuous and at many levels. By so viewing it, we recognize that all aspects of his experience are not equally available to man, but that, whatever the degree of consciousness, awareness is an essential part of man's being.[6]

The human mind is seen to have the capacity of free choice, from which the humanistic psychologist derives the idea of man's capability for change. Bugental continues:

> Phenomenologically, choice is a given of experience. When man is aware, he is aware that his choices make a difference in the flow of his awareness, that he is not a bystander but a participant in experience.[7]

2. *Man has worth.* Since man is more than matter, each individual is inherently worthwhile and not merely a piece of the universe. The humanistic psychologist rejects the mechanism and "thing-like" overtones of materialistic psychologies. He also rejects the Freudian view of personality as being the battleground for biological instincts and unconscious forces. Rather, each person is unique as a thinker, feeler, and creator. Each individual, not abstract man, is studied. A person and his experience is the subject matter of this psychology.

3. *Man has potential.* The human being is obviously a very powerful being as master of the planet and has much unused potential for good, change, and adaptation. Look at his cultural and intellectual achievements, all in spite of many historical handicaps such as war and disease. The humanistic psychologist predicts that this potential residing in each human will send him to heights of success and enjoyment he has never known before.

4. *Man is good.* The humanistic world view says that at his core man is motivated toward good behavior, i.e., toward that which is good for himself and others. Abraham Maslow taught this principle of the goodness of man in the following passage:

> As far as I know we just don't have any intrinsic instincts for evil. If you think in terms of the basic needs; instincts, at least at the outset, are all "good"—or perhaps we should be technical about it and call them "pre-moral," neither good nor evil. We do know, however, that out of the search for fulfillment of a basic need—take love in the child for example—can come evil. The child, wanting his mother's exclusive love, may bash his little brother over the head in hopes of getting more of it. What we call evil or pathological

may certainly arise from, or replace, something good. Another example is the little squabbles among children; all the fighting they do about who should do what, about dividing up the chores, ultimately can be seen as a distorted expression of a very powerful need for fairness and justice.[8]

Humans have always wondered whether in their inner beings they have been driven to good or to evil. Humanistic thinkers reject Freud's picture of man's inner drives being aimed toward physical satisfaction and aggression. They also reject Skinner's view of a passive inner nature that can be shaped toward good or evil depending on the contingencies of reinforcement in the environment.

The humanistic psychologist does not say that all humans are perfect, but he does say they have the potential for human perfection. The purpose of each person, then, is to reach full potential and become fully human. According to this thinking, man is not just motivated to survive but to become better and better. This process of continual improvement is called self-actualization. It is a process in which, as basic physiological needs (hunger, thirst, sex) are met, the person is freed to meet his higher needs of affection, security, and esteem. These are human growth needs and when fulfilled should culminate in a state of being self-actualized.

A self-actualized person can be loosely described as one who is using his or her talents and capabilities to the fullest. The negative criterion is an absence of tendencies toward psychological problems, or mental illness. The self-actualized person is the best possible specimen of the human species, a representative of what Maslow later came to call the "growing tip." Such a person, he felt, represented the true nature of humanity.

HUMANISTIC PSYCHOLOGY

The Nature of Man's Problems

The humanistic psychologist is not blind to the many personal and social problems that have always plagued humanity. Speaking of the potential for self-actualized health and happiness, Frank Goble gives the humanistic explanation for the fact that so few, if any, people achieve this human potential:

> In spite of the fact that apparently all have this potential, only a tiny percentage is now achieving it. This is, in part, because people are blind to their potential; they neither know what is possible nor understand the rewards of self-actualization.[9]

The ultimate reason, then, for our unsolved problems—personal mental weakness, crime, anger, etc.—is an ignorance, or a lack of use, of inner potential to overcome these problems. Therefore, humanistic psychologists seek to employ techniques in education, business, politics, and the counseling office to unlock the life-changing human potential.

Other reasons that humans fail to grow to their full psychological potential are suggested by humanistic psychologists:[10]

1. Man's instincts toward growth are weak and can be stifled by habits, environment, and poor education.
2. Western culture teaches us to fear our instincts, and this suppresses and controls human growth.
3. Our needs of safety and security restrain us from seeking higher growth needs.
4. We fear our highest possibilities and lack the courage to step into them.
5. Our culture stifles growth of character traits such as sympathy, kindness, gentleness, and tenderness.

The Nature of Solutions

By what we have covered of this world view, we see that the solutions proposed for all types of problems are structured by the humanistic view of man and the nature of his problems. The general solution is for man to discover himself and thus develop his potential. Humanness needs to be developed. Altruism and the like are not character traits that one just falls into, but they must be resolutely cultivated, and a coming to maturity is required before they become a reality.

In the solution of psychological problems counseling techniques are used to explore and to encourage self. There is a great emphasis on strengthening one's self-image; on increasing a person's use of that which is human through sensitivity sessions and encounter groups; and on nondirective, empathic counseling to rid the self of limiting guilt. Carl Rogers's client-centered therapy is a prime example of these approaches.

In the realm of education, classrooms are "opened"; and instead of the traditional lecture method, there can be the exploration of feelings and speculations on academic matters. The purpose of humanistic educators is not to teach facts per se but to teach us to explore ourselves and to become better persons. One does not learn about child psychology experiments but rather learns to become a better parent.

For society's ills Maslow proposed "Eupsychia," his version of a utopia, which could be achieved by well, self-actualized adults and children. People in such a society, rather than protecting themselves from their natural instincts as the Freudians attempted to get clients to do, would create an environment where people would follow their instincts and satisfy their innate psychological needs. "Maslow envisions a society with psychologically healthy people where there will be less crime, less mental illness, less need for restrictive legislation."[11]

THE POSITIVE CONTRIBUTIONS OF HUMANISTIC PSYCHOLOGY

In summary, the humanistic world view contains much truth, and it is important to recognize the accuracy of many of its contributions to psychological thought.

1. The whole person is studied by the humanistic psychologists, who use a mixture of scientific and phenomenological methods.
2. Counseling is humanized because the individual is extremely worthwhile to the humanistic psychologist.
3. Reductionism in man is rejected.
4. Human problems are studied, and instead of brains and muscles, these become the prime objects of research concern.

Humanistic psychology, though, does have its share of problems as a world view. These will be discussed in the next chapter.

. . . his propensity for wickedness is something more than merely evidence of unrealized potential . . . it is a demonstration that something has gone dreadfully wrong from which there now seems no possibility of self recovery.

Arthur Custance

A HUMANISTIC SAND CASTLE

One of the more serious limitations of the view of the humanistic psychologist is that he builds his view of human nature on a presuppositional basis that will not support a lofty view of man. That basis is a naturalistic view of origins and nature. According to naturalistic thinking, all in the universe, including man, has arrived via time + matter + energy + chance. The problem for the humanistic psychologist is to get personality from the impersonal universe. This is not just a biological problem that will some day be solved. Trying to draw more from nature than it has to give demands a suspension of logic that scientists make in no other part of their work except evolutionary discontinuities such as life evolving from nonlife and consciousness from matter. One gets the correct impression that this thinking is a presuppositional leap and not a scientific conclusion from the world of data.

Furthermore, what makes a person more valuable than a rock or a cow? In an impersonal universe, personality might be an unwanted freak of nature, especially personality that destroys the ecology of nature, builds bombs, and lives in emotional anguish. One might ask why we cannot ignore this inconsistency and say that man is valuable, but we have no basis for saying so when we hold this world view. This inconsistent thinking hides intellectual dishonesty and the fact that there is error in one's world view. Either man is not so "human" and valuable, or nature is not just material. There is a tendency to search for inner consistency in a view of life. Francis Schaeffer describes those whose presuppositions do not fit the world in which they live:

> Every person feels the pull of two consistencies, the pull towards the real world and the pull towards the logic of his system. He may let the pendulum swing back and forth be-

tween them, but he cannot live in both places at once. He will be living nearer to the one or to the other, depending on the strengths of the pull at any given time. To have to choose between one consistency or the other is a real damnation for man. *The more logical a man is to his own presuppositions, the further he is from the real world; and the nearer he is to the real world, the more illogical he is to his presuppositions.* [1] (emphasis his)

The logician says to us that matter cannot rise above itself to become a living human being. The real world of data and experience says that man, with his mind and nobility, really exists. The humanistic psychologist is pulled toward both of these concepts, but he cannot hold to both. This means that the humanistic psychologist is pressured, on the one hand, to keep his naturalistic assumptions about the universe and thus to lower man to a biological machine. On the other hand, he is pressured by the reality of his world to change his naturalistic presuppositions in order to provide a basis for the reality of human nature. The glorious age of humanism and the glories of the human being turned quickly into the age of naturalism and empiricism and the abolition of human nature because men chose the naturalistic route. We will see that most humanistic psychologists have drifted toward the latter route. They have, however, changed some world-view assumptions about nature by embracing Eastern concepts about reality found in transpersonal psychology. Through these concepts nature is elevated, and thus the discontinuity between man and nature is avoided.

HUMANISTIC PSYCHOLOGY AND THE "FLAW" IN HUMAN NATURE

In an effort to testify to the dignity, worth, and value of man—qualities that are indeed evident, humanistic psychology ignores the legion of evidences that man has a character flaw at the core of his being.

We find both good and evil people in the world, and the humanistic psychologist holds that the goodness is a result of their following the instincts of their inner natures. While people have much potential for good, it appears that they have another part besides goodness, which includes other instincts, if you will, that war against goodness. In fact, when we find goodness in individuals, it appears to be more the result of cultural restraints, such as law and civilization, than the result of giving freedom to man's inner impulses.

When restraints to human instincts are removed, such as in times of a local emergency during a flood or a war, we see the worst traits of man emerge. Anthropologist Arthur Custance, after a careful, scientific analysis of the problem of bad behavior in people, declared the following:

> We are not really more sinful or less sinful, but more restrained or less restrained, i.e., more cultured or less so. In short, the concept of the innocence of childhood requires some careful redefinition, and if by such innocence is meant innate goodness, it is a mistaken view of human nature. The innocence of childhood results rather from lack of time and opportunity to realize the inborn potential for wickedness than for some natural tendency in the opposite direction. . . .
>
> While it is perhaps true that a slum environment breeds crime, it does so because it provides more opportunity for inherently sinful human nature to express itself, social restraints being greatly reduced.[2]

This was a theme in Golding's *Lord of the Flies*, in which polite, proper, young British schoolboys turned into murdering savages when they were lost on a tropical island. It is true that some individuals develop good, internal restraints and are reasonably good and law-abiding people even in stressful situations; but the point is that we are always compelled to restrain our inner natures in order to produce the maximum good. Why is it so difficult to seek another's good and so easy to think of self? B. F. Skinner would say that the environment rewards one for good or for bad behavior. Yet it seems more accurate to say that environment speeds up or slows down a process of "self-drive" that is operative in everyone.

Another point to consider is that so few, if any, individuals reach the personal potential described by the humanistic psychologist as self-actualization. Indeed, persons who are nearly self-actualized are evidence of this potential in man, but the humanistic psychologist fails to explain why people do not reach this potential. Maslow himself admits that there are few, if any, of these self-actualized individuals to be found. Speaking of Maslow's search for self-actualized individuals, Frank Goble says:

> The individuals he studied were selected from his personal acquaintances and friends, from public figures, living and dead, and selected college students. In the first attempt with young people, two thousand college students were considered, but only one sufficiently mature individual was found.[3]

Without the evidence that there are a great many self-actualized individuals, all we can conclude is that we have evidence for such potential in man, but not that he can ever reach this potential of fulfillment and altruism. Self-actualization, or the potential for goodness, is an unrealized assumption and not the source of a systematic observation of the real world. Man has the potential for goodness, but yet he seems held back from ever totally realizing his potential.

People also seem to be weak psychologically. Maslow admits that the reason we don't often see people's higher aspirations achieved is that they are very weak instincts when compared to their biological instincts. A person is often a victim of his biological drives, and, in the language of Freud, the id is the master of the ego. Or as B. F. Skinner might say it, "We are controlled by physically reinforcing stimuli." I do not believe that the will has to be mastered by the physical drives, but why does it demand such a war to conquer them, if any of us ever do conquer them? The inner self seems weak and not strong.

One theory in social psychology well illustrates this point. The theory of cognitive dissonance, put forward by Leon Festinger, is that an individual will tend to change his beliefs in order to fit his actions. [4] For this reason a smoker is less likely to believe that cigarettes cause cancer than a nonsmoker does. For a smoker to believe strongly that his actions will cause cancer is to admit, "I am a dummy," or "I am too weak to quit," both admissions being damaging to his self-image. Therefore, to protect self, a person unconsciously changes his view of reality and his criteria for evaluating the evidence on smoking and cancer. He then says, "I don't think the cancer reports are valid," or "I don't smoke enough to be harmed." This process of cognitive dissonance seems to operate in everyone. But why? Why do we try to change reality to protect self?

This internal self-protection process also contributes to mental illness when a person finds reality too difficult to bear and thus changes his views about reality. For example, consider the defense mechanism of rationalization. When a student gets a low grade on a test for which he did not study, he begins to believe that the teacher is out to get him. He has distorted reality to protect self. When there is enough of a distortion of reality during severe circumstances so that a person is not in contact with the real world at all, such a situation is labeled a *psychosis*. Again, in such a case there is a process at work that seems to be a restraining influence on the development of a healthy personality.

People also seem to lack purpose and meaning in life, even in the face of apparent satisfaction of their physiological and higher needs. Abraham Maslow's hierarchy of needs—of body, safety, love, esteem, and self-actualization—probably does not describe all of the needs of a human being if he is to be fulfilled. The existential psychologists Rollo May and Victor Frankl point this out and add that the inner fear of nonbeing (death) plagues us all. We have a need for spiritual certainty. This was stated by Victor Frankl:

> Is psychology prepared to deal with the present need? Above all I consider it dangerous to press man's search for meaning into stereotype interpretations such as "nothing but defense mechanisms" or "secondary rationalizations." I think that man's quest for, and even his questioning of a meaning to his existence, i.e., his spiritual aspirations as well as his spiritual frustrations should be taken at face value and should not be tranquilized or analyzed away.[5]

It is as if humans have a capacity for life that is not met in this present life. For example, many people openly admit a lack of spiritual reality in their lives and an alienation from God. It is alienation from a God who fulfills a true human need that is historic Christianity's explanation for man's having self-interest at the center of his being and for his resultant bent toward evil.

A HUMANISTIC SAND CASTLE

Related to this idea that there are unmet needs in man is the evidence of the transpersonal psychologist, who in studying meditative and hallucinogenic experiences says that there are higher levels of awareness from which man seems cut off. We can compare man to a jet plane that is restricted to operating in two dimensions, length and width (on the ground), when it was made to move also in a third (in the air). It might be said that the jet makes a superior kind of "automobile" on the highway, just as man makes a very successful animal. However, when one looks at the wings and the big engines of the jet, he gets the impression that it was made to fly. So, too, when we see the enormous potential of a human to experience and think, we begin to wonder if he has not fallen from a higher existence than that of being merely the highest in the animal kingdom. To say that he is evolving toward this potential ignores the fact that these needs and longings in humans have always been observed, fully developed. Primitive cavemen were, perhaps, more concerned with spiritual gods and life after death than we are today. The transpersonal psychologist feels that man is "cut off" from spiritual life and knowledge. This is another good description of the defective nature of man.

A final point concerning man's defective inner character is that it seems to be true that a great deal of the resistance to belief in the "sin nature" in man comes from humanistic counselors, who in building up the case for goodness in people, reject any discussion that makes them out to be less than perfect. No one wishes to deny the marvelous good and potential in people, but the evidence does point to the other side of their natures as well, and we need to recognize this evidence.

There seems to be a resistance by many humanistic counselors to deal with the subject of fault, or guilt, in counseling because they think it can have negative effects on the development of a positive self-image and an autonomous sense of self-direction in the client. In addition, if we find fault with ourselves, this is a hint there is absolute right and wrong, an idea that the humanistic relativist seeks to avoid.

We must deal realistically in counseling situations. To ignore selfish motives and behavior in order to protect a person's ego is to do a disservice to the client in the long run if selfish life patterns adversely affect mental health. This does not mean that every counseling problem has bad behavior as its roots, but many persons seek a counselor for relief of guilt feelings arising from true guilt. It is reasonable to suggest that counseling can take place in a gentle and loving fashion and yet deal with irresponsible behavior without raising more guilt feelings.[6]

All of the above evidences suggest that all may not be well in the inner being of man. As we turn within, in our experience, we find our natures wishing to do well but powerless to always achieve the good. This problem with the inner self has led many in the humanistic movement, including Maslow himself, to seek new and more powerful techniques, not only to release the inner potential of people but also to transform or transcend this self-potential. This problem is also a reason for the humanistic psychologist's searching in transpersonal psychology for such answers and techniques.

EXPERIENCE AND TRUTH

Another area of concern that many scientists have with humanistic psychology is its emphasis on subjective experience. Psychologist Gary Collins voices this concern:

> Freed by their own self-definition from disciplined intellectual precision or scientific rigor, the humanists have built an existential experience-based system which rests on the debatable assumption that total psychic transparency and self-exposure will lead to therapeutic and growth-releasing potential. By de-emphasizing intellectual and reasoning abilities, the humanists have put themselves in danger of reducing man to an experience-directed being who may have freedom but who certainly is without dignity.[7]

It is all right to include subjective experience as subject matter in psychology and to study our inner experiences, but we cannot set up experience as our criterion for truth. The humanistic psychologist is often more interested in what his client thinks or feels about something than in absolute truth. For example, what one feels is a valid sexual encounter becomes truth for him or her. This, of course, ends any discussion of absolute truth in the counseling office or the classroom.

We see two results in this type of thinking. One is the "playing around" appearance of humanistic psychology. Everyone has heard of the "touchie-feelie" groups and the encounter groups. Their purpose is to increase one's awareness (physical and psychological sensitivity) of the world around him. However, the negative result of experience for experience' sake is that it can and does become an end in itself, only fun and games. But of course, play is one of the signs of a healthy person to the humanistic psychologist. There is nothing wrong with play, but psychological wholeness comes from truth first of all. All play and no truth can make psychology an ineffective therapeutic field.

A second result of thinking of experience as truth

is the emphasis on feelings to the complete avoidance of behavioral or cognitive factors in the counseling situation. Certainly our loving concern for patients should lead us to help relieve their disturbed emotions. But when having good feelings or the venting of negative emotions becomes the goal of the counseling appointment, we are not working to solve the problems that produced the bad feelings. *We also lose our right to question any behavior that results in good feelings.* Imagine that Adolf Hitler had sought counseling for feeling depressed and that his counselor had asked him when the last time was that he had felt good. Hitler might have answered that he had felt good when he had conquered Poland. Should he then have been advised to attack England?

Because of the humanistic psychologist's view, he is not allowed to develop guidance in counseling except concerning the relativity of a patient's experience and feelings. There is much evidence that counseling regarding the thinking and behavior patterns of clients, as well as regarding their emotions, is desirable.[8] It is interesting that a movement that begins as a praise and elevation for what is human gradually trades in the rational man for the emotional man.

In conclusion, in this chapter we have seen the humanistic psychologist in rebellion against the excessive materialism of naturalistic psychology. But he finds himself on the horns of a dilemma. How does he justify the existence of people's minds and personalities when the material universe cannot produce them? The dilemma forces him either to believe in naturalistic psychology and scientific and logical credibility or to change the materialistic presupposition concerning nature so that he can build a

A HUMANISTIC SAND CASTLE

7

The child says, oh look, Mommy, a purple cow, and the mother says, there is no such thing as a purple cow, sweetheart, and so the kid stops reporting purple cows, and gradually as he gets older the visual messages processed by his brain are modified and translated in terms of Mommy's world until he can't remember seeing a purple cow. (The purple cows then walk around with impunity, unseen by anyone.)

Adam Smith

TRANSPERSONAL PSYCHOLOGY

The last world view in psychology that we will cover (before considering Christian theism) is known as transpersonal psychology, often called the fourth force in psychology.[1] It involves the current study of expanded consciousness and the spiritual nature of people through drugs, meditation, biofeedback, deep hypnosis, ESP, the occult, deathbed experiences, and Eastern religions. The first issue of *The Journal of Transpersonal Psychology* defined the field of transpersonal psychology in the statement of purpose in 1969:

> *The Journal of Transpersonal Psychology* is concerned with . . . metaneeds, ultimate values, unitive consciousness, peak experiences, ecstasy, mystical experience, B values, essence, bliss, awe, wonder, self-actualization, ultimate meaning, transcendence of the self, spirit, sacralization of everyday life, oneness, cosmic awareness, cosmic play, individual and species-wide synergy, maximal interpersonal encounter, transcendental phenomena, maximal sensory awareness, responsiveness and expression, and related concepts, experiences and activities.[2]

In later issues of the journal the practices of meditation and other spiritual paths are added. The term *transpersonal* is used because the transpersonal psychological world view recognizes the need for the person to transcend his present consciousness and thereby achieve higher states of "true" awareness than are normally possible.

These transpersonal subjects entered into psychology early through the interests of William James, Carl Jung, and Aldous Huxley. More recently Abraham Maslow, with his emphasis on peak experiences, entered the field. Maslow did much for the new emphasis on transpersonal psychology, and this was no accident since by humanistic, psychological methods human nature was not taken as far as its potential would allow. Abraham Maslow, in the first public presentation of the fourth force in psychology, said,

> Thus we are using techniques for selecting the most fully developed, the most fully human persons we can find and suggesting that these people are what the whole human species can be like if you just let them grow, if the conditions are good and you get out of their way.[3]

Thus, we can conclude that transpersonal psychology has emerged largely from humanistic psychology.[4] In transpersonal psychology there seemed to be a way to emphasize elements of man that could change him. Maslow reported peak experiences in which a person is in a moment of bliss, egoless, beyond time and space and good and evil; and he observed that this state is similar to that of some who were reporting under the influence of drugs or were meditating.

The experiences that people have had in these altered-consciousness states have led to questions about the whole nature of man and reality. This is important because we see in this brand of psychology the beginnings of change in some of the most cherished, Western, scientific, naturalistic presuppositions. The emphasis, in this psychology, is not on physical reality but on the psychical reality of experience.

The basis for interest in recent fads such as hallucinogenic drug trips and transcendental meditation is that they are used to unveil supposed uncharted realities and so are looked upon as methods to actually enter these realities. The uncharted regions of the mind are being studied, not only by the Timothy Learys but by serious scientists from many backgrounds. R. D. Laing, a British psychoanalyst, is a prime example. In treating psychotic patients experiencing extreme ego loss, he discovered that many such patients were undergoing experiences similar to those described by mystics. Laing felt that what we have commonly been calling insanity may actually be a break in ordinary consciousness leading to richer perception and fuller functioning.[5]

Many Western men and women have demanded some spiritual answers and peace of mind amid their technological pollution, and they are looking to the East and the presuppositions found there about reality. However, being unwilling to pack up and move to India, they attempt to combine their familiar Western world view with Eastern techniques, and thus their explanation of reality becomes half East, half West. As one would expect, such a composite view has its problems.

Transpersonal thinking is also at the basis of new developments in psychology such as Gestalt therapy and Structural Integration, the Esalen Institute, Zen tennis, yoga exercises, and Sufism.

Let us look at the transpersonal world view. Again, it is hard to create a category that fits everyone in a certain world view, and this is especially true of transpersonal psychology, in which so many viewpoints are permitted.

In spite of the difficulty in categorizing these viewpoints, however, one thing is certain. The transpersonal psychologist is proposing a radically altered way of looking at reality and people. The following are some statements regarding a growing revolution exhibited in transpersonal ways of thinking:

> We are, in fact, caught between two competing world views. The crisis in America, the generation gap, the counter culture, is a reflection of a shift in world view that is happening to a significant minority within our population.[6]

Psychologists are people of their culture, and our particular culture is in the midst of profound change. There exists a "countercultural" community opposed to science, exhibiting a tremendous distaste for rational thought.[7]

THE MAJOR COMPONENTS OF TRANSPERSONAL PSYCHOLOGY

The Nature of Reality

To the transpersonal psychologist reality is "two-headed," one head represented by the Western view of a physical, orderly world, and the other head by the Eastern view of the spiritual oneness of reality. On the Western side we have stars, planets, people, and atoms, all ruled by principles of cause and effect. On the Eastern side we have universal mind and spiritual substance, which operate by noncausal principles, infusing all matter. The noncausal principles of this spiritual side of the universe give rise to magical, coincidental, and illogical effects.

Actually, the transpersonal psychologist does not see two separate realities in the universe but only a continuum, with the two realities merging into one another in the middle. Arthur Koestler, in his book *The Roots of Coincidence,* feels that particle physics may represent the joining ground of matter and nonmatter.[8] He says, "It is not always easy to draw a sharp line separating causal from non-causal events."[9] As we dig deeper into the nature of matter, according to this view, we find matter composed of particles that seem to border on nonmatter.

Both the universe and its contents are seen by the transpersonal psychologist as separate entities and as an interconnected, whole essence also. This is especially true of human nature: the transpersonal psychologist sees the individual personality of man and yet he also sees that man participates in the essence and oneness of all things.

The current thinking of the transpersonal psychologist is beginning to sound more Eastern than Western. It is as if he is beginning to doubt the reality of the physical universe, or at least its importance. What goes on *in mind* is more important than the physical, scientific world *out there*, i.e., there is physical reality, but psychical reality is more important than physical reality. Some even go so far as to say that psychical reality creates our experiences of what we call physical reality, and thus only psychical reality exists. Charles Tart, editor of the book *Transpersonal Psychologies*, said:

> Because my ability to predict what will happen in the class of experiences I attribute to the external world is so remarkably high (I know that every time I walk into the experience I call a closed door, I will have the experience I call a bumped nose), I have come, like everyone else, to believe that the physical world exists independently of my experience of it, but that belief says something about my psychology, not necessarily anything about the ultimate nature of reality.[10]

To the transpersonal psychologist, knowing is both through science—the study of the physical, cause-effect world—and through altered conscious experience, which is supposedly experiencing reality directly. Tart again says:

> We *are* twentieth-century Westerners, with science in general and scientific psychology in particular as important parts of our backgrounds. Some of us may be able to drop that background and accept a particular transpersonal psychology as our primary frame of reference. But for many of us, what we learn about the spiritual side of ourselves must at least coexist with, and preferably *integrate with*, our heritage of Western science and culture. So I think our job will be to bridge the spiritual and our Western, scientific side.[11]

Experiential knowledge may be available during meditation, dreams, hallucinogenic drug trips, or by revelation, or sudden intuition. All of these produce a type of knowing that is difficult to describe. The reader has experienced similar forms of "knowing" during those transitional states between waking and sleeping called hypnogogic states. Some evening before retiring or during a bout with sleep in a boring classroom hold a pencil between two fingers so that you will drop it the moment you fall asleep. The pencil's falling will awaken you during a hypnogogic state, which is not really a dream. You will recall having unusual stream-of-consciousness ideas, which are holistic rather than sequential, as in our normal thought patterns. These hypnogogic thoughts are difficult to express in words, and yet they are ideas nonetheless. A hypnogogic state may be a far cry from the depth of experience during a meditative state but will give you an idea of what an intuitive mode of knowing might be like.

There are, then, two modes of knowing: the rational, sequential, and verbal and the intuitive, spatial, and diffuse. The intuitive mode of thought and experience is seen as the prime data in transpersonal psychology, whereas physiology and behavior are merely secondary sources of data. Transpersonal psychologist Robert Ornstein says, "Psychology is, primarily, the science of human experience. Its researchers study secondary phenomena—such as behavior, physiology, and 'verbal report'—as they relate to crucial questions of consciousness."[12]

The Nature of Man

Man is seen as a creature that is composed of both matter and mind. However, many transpersonal psychologists, in emphasizing the mind and experience,

TRANSPERSONAL PSYCHOLOGY

say that matter is an illusion, created by the mind's limited perception of reality.

The transpersonal psychologist believes that in evolutionary history the human brain evolved as an information reducer and as an analyzer of the real world. The brain, in other words, reduces the amount of sense information available to a minimum since it cannot handle all of this information. Therefore, we miss a genuine portion of reality. The brain screens out cosmic rays, ultraviolet light, high frequency sound, and most of the nonphysical, unity nature of the universe.

In order to survive during the early stages of evolution, man needed to concentrate on seeing lions and tigers, and therefore he now sees lions and tigers. Frogs, needing to see less to survive, have evolved to see only small, moving bugs.[13] But, according to the transpersonal thinker, the human of today needs to open up to more of reality in order to experience life fully. The human brain, as an analyzer, concentrates on perceiving physical reality and on breaking it up into separate, discrete items of reality. It analyzes nature into pieces instead of seeing the unity and oneness that is really there.

Language and world view also play parts and act as screens or filters to what the human is able to perceive. Words limit his thinking processes, and his beliefs structure what he is willing to look for in reality. With all of these things considered, the transpersonal psychologist sees the human in a big universe with a perceiving apparatus that takes in only a select portion of reality. He is at a low level of cosmic awareness. He cannot "see" the spiritual nature of things; he cannot "see" the essential oneness of things; he cannot "see" the interrelationships of life; he cannot "see" his place in the universe.

However, humans do have the potential to expand their awareness. According to the transpersonal psychologist, the right hemisphere of the human brain gives us a clue that man needs to expand his perceptions of reality.[14] The dominant, left half of the brain seems to perceive things analytically and logically, especially in the areas of verbal and mathematical functioning. Its mode of operation is sequential. Logic, language, and math depend on such sequential processing.

The right, nondominant hemisphere, on the other hand, seems specialized for synthesis, i.e., for seeing the holistic and relational nature of things. The right hemisphere is limited in language ability and seems to be more creative and intuitive in its information processing than the left hemisphere is. Therefore, the transpersonal psychologist says, man must be educated in this intuitive mode of thought. He must have his consciousness altered to permit him to be more aware of the nature of reality.

The Nature of Man's Problems

Man's condition is obvious at this point. He has a level of consciousness that restricts or distorts reality. In the real world, according to transpersonal thought, things are "one" on a spiritual level. It is such reality that man must be made aware of. There are no major attempts to relate this limitation in awareness in man to man's behavior, though there is some suggestion that a loss of an "I-it" way of thinking would help solve strained personal relationships and the ecological crisis.

Man's problem is also that he exists too much as a separate self-identity. He is an individual person in his behavior, but in reality he is one with many persons and things. The Eastern techniques are designed to make one lose this sense of self, which has obviously been so disadvantageous in the "selfish" Western society with its wars, capitalistic greed, and ecological rape of nature.

The reason for man's condition is not agreed on in the camp of transpersonal thinkers. One suggestion is that man suffers from a low consciousness level because of incomplete evolution. He is on his way "up" to higher levels of consciousness. The animal world represents a continuum of consciousness, from a creature like the amoeba to creatures with species consciousness like army ants, to conscious monkeys, to the self-conscious human. The next step "up" for the human is cosmic consciousness and the loss of personality.

Another idea, expressed in an article on Arica Training (which is a transpersonal training institute) in a section entitled "Assumptions Inherently Unprovable," John Lilly and Joseph Hart assume that children are born with a higher consciousness but that they lose it in the process of living:

> When a child is born he is pure essence: a natural being in an ordered cosmos, one with all men and with God, instinctive, loving. This is the perfect state of innocence, but the child must grow. Under the influence of his surroundings, parents, society, he begins to develop a personality for survival, the ego, between four to six years of age. The awareness of the joy and harmony of his essence dims until he is conscious only of his ego, which is fighting for survival in a threatening world. This lack of awareness of the essence leads to the unhappiness which many feel as part of man's condition in this world.[15]

The Nature of Solutions

The solutions to man's low level of consciousness are the myriad techniques used to produce altered states of consciousness. Three of the most popular techniques are meditation, biofeedback, and hallucinogenic drugs. All produce expanded awareness. Meditation produces a sense of peace and serenity and a floating, oceanic feeling. This is the cosmic consciousness experience or the feeling of oneness with the universe. The gaining of the virtues so often associated with the Eastern meditator—such as humility, quietness, or bodily control—is not the goal of life but only part of the technique used to produce expanded consciousness.

LSD, an artificial or synthetic chemical, and mescaline, a chemical found in buttons on the peyote cactus, are two of the more common "mind-expanding" drugs. They are known to produce vivid hallucinations and "oneness with reality" experiences. We are not exactly sure why these drugs have their effects. They may mimic brain transmitters and thus alter brain activity, or they may destroy reality by altering the logical sequence of "framing" in one's stream-of-consciousness. Another suggestion is that these drugs temporarily suppress the usual dominance of the major brain hemisphere and allow reality to be processed primarily through the nonlogical minor hemisphere.

Since the alpha brain waves are known to be correlated with states of deep meditation, biofeedback has become popular as a "shortcut" to altered consciousness. When a person is in a relaxed state of mind, with his eyes closed, much of his cortex shows alpha waves, cycles of brain activity, of ten to twelve per second. A skilled meditator develops voluntary control over his brain states. To develop such control, however, is a long, learning process involving increased awareness of inner, psychic states. The advantage of biofeedback is that an individual gets direct, auditory feedback of his current alpha state

TRANSPERSONAL PSYCHOLOGY

monitored by an electroencephalograph (EEG). With this feedback a person learns what to think or not to think in order to produce more alpha waves, and this allows him to achieve the same sort of alpha control as a meditator does. Biofeedback enthusiasts describe this alpha state as being similar to a mild "drug high."

Any psychological world view, if it is to find acceptance, must have application in the lives of its adherents. Transpersonal psychologists know this and are seeking to apply the esoteric doctrines of panpsychism and Eastern religious techniques to the psychological problems of modern man. The exact nature of counseling techniques to sprout from the transpersonal psychological world view is being much discussed by transpersonal thinkers.[16]

To the transpersonal therapist it is not so clear that the psychotic or the schizophrenic is "sick." The reason is that the inner experiences of the mentally ill are similar to mystical experiences. To the transpersonal thinker the loss of ego identity and even the visual and auditory hallucinations may be desirable, and the patient's experience needs to be understood in this context. The patient needs help in understanding his experience and not impersonal therapeutic measures that make him think of himself as odd or sick.

In addition, everyone in our Western society is seen by the transpersonal psychologist as needing transpersonal psychotherapy since everyone suffers problems in self-control, personal relationships, and meaning in life; and society itself suffers from war, pollution, crime, and greed. The transpersonal experience of oneness with ultimate reality, our fellow humans, and nature is seen as the basic psychotherapeutic solution.

It is not difficult to imagine then that future transpersonal therapists will be offering their clients training in the mind-expanding techniques as well as counseling help to change the Western presuppositions they have learned and their preconceived views of reality that cause them to be out of touch with reality. The goal of such counseling sessions would be a more peaceful, egoless existence for the mentally and emotionally disturbed.

NATURALISTIC AND TRANSPERSONAL ASSUMPTIONS COMPARED

Let us continue this discussion of the transpersonal world view with a contrast of the naturalistic and transpersonal presuppositions. We will then examine these presuppositions to see how they are used to prejudice the psychologists' interpretations of various experiential phenomena.

Naturalistic Psychology	Transpersonal Psychology
1. Reality is the physical world.	Reality is the psychical world of experience.
2. The present moment is all that exists.	Time is not a linear construct.
3. Man is only matter.	Man is both body and mind.
4. Man is an individual locked inside his nervous system.	Man is a part of nature and has a spiritual or psychic connection with it.
5. Brain gives rise to consciousness.	Brain transmits consciousness.
6. Man is born new except for genetic inheritance.	Man can bring an inheritance of mind from other lives.
7. Everything has evolved by blind chance.	Evolution is guided by nonphysical forces.

8. Psychological en- ergy comes from physiological energy.	Psychical energy exists.
9. Man's purpose is to have immediate pleasure or to conquer nature; or he has no purpose at all.	Man's purpose is to become more conscious than he is.
10. Death is the end of the personality.	We survive physical death in some form of consciousness.
11. The loss of sense of self is mental illness.	Losing personality (self) is a goal, i.e., gaining union with the universe.
12. Reasoning is man's highest skill.	Intuition is man's highest skill.

Now let us examine the various psychological phenomena along with the proposed explanations of these phenomena by the naturalistic and transpersonal psychologists.

The Mystic Experience

Under the effects of hallucinogenic drugs or of meditation a person reports a feeling of peacefulness, vivid sensations, the loss of a sense of time, and an oceanic feeling or loss of the sense of self. The person begins to feel joined to, or at one with, the desk next to him.

1. *Naturalistic explanation.* First of all, there is no direct way to verify the subject's report of this experience. It is his private experience. We could attach an EEG to his head and try to observe his brain waves. The drug must be increasing or decreasing neuron firing in his brain, thus explaining the vivid sensations; the drug could also cause certain neurons to

form new, unusual associations with other neurons, thus producing distortions in sensory input. Our sense of self requires incoming sensory input from all of our senses, and meditation screens out this needed sensory input, producing a loss of sense of the physical self, and hence the "oneness experience" with the desk occurs.

2. *Transpersonal explanation.* When a person sees brightness and lights and senses a oneness with a desk, he is seeing the universe the way it really is. Ordinarily, his brain screens input, structures time, and analyzes sense data into discrete elements, but this only serves to give him an erroneous sense of individuality. When the mind is altered, or "opened up," he begins to see the true world. He *is* a part of the desk. Time *is* only an arbitrary structure.

Parapsychology

In parapsychology, or ESP, we find reports of phenomena such as telepathy (awareness of what is in another's mind), clairvoyance (awareness of an object without the use of the senses), precognition (awareness of something in the future), and telekinesis (mind over matter). How can we explain these phenomena?

1. *Naturalistic explanation.* Again, many or all of these phenomena may not exist except as mistaken or fraudulent reports. If they are authentic, a process such as subliminal perception may be taking place, by which a normal stimulus is below the conscious threshold but is unconsciously received anyway. Perhaps there are special waves being transmitted from one brain to the next—a phenomenon we may one day discover. However, researchers have failed to isolate such waves and in fact have shown that the

supposed extrasensory transmission does not get weaker with transmission distance as it should if it were a physical phenomenon.

2. *Transpersonal explanation.* One possible explanation is that there are brain waves that do not obey normal physical laws, such as psychic waves or *psi* particles. Another reasonable explanation is that humans at their subconscious level are linked to all other people in a collective unconscious.[17] After all, we are one with all things in the universe. Paranormal phenomena seem to occur best when the conscious mind is relaxed, or in an unconscious trance or dream state. Reading a mind is merely being aware of thoughts through the subconscious connection. Since it is true that all is one and that we are one with people and things over space and time, we can explain an awareness of objects and events, past, present, and future, since they are really a part of our own reality.

Out-of-Body Travel

We hear reports of out-of-body travel, most often associated with deathbed experiences.[18] People who had clinically died and were resuscitated report leaving their bodies and meeting with spirits.

1. *Naturalistic explanation.* These experiences happen only in people's minds. How they know of events out of their sight and hearing is not known by scientists. We have to run better experiments to control other variables during these experiences. The same experiences that happen on the supposed deathbed also happen on other occasions, such as when people have been drugged or have nearly drowned, times when the people obviously have not died and gone to heaven. Saying that I have experi-

enced heaven is not the most reasonable nor the most cautious explanation.

2. *Transpersonal explanation.* The human has a nonphysical body, which is set free at death. Many individuals learn to travel in it. An individual does not have to die to experience this out-of-body travel and communication with other spirits.

As one can see, there is very little communication going on between the naturalist and the transpersonalist. Each sees the world through his own world view and has an explanation for almost everything. It is very difficult to imagine any data at this point that would convince either to accept the other's position. We are definitely living in an age when communication is breaking down between scientists because they are ignorant of their own presuppositions and those of their colleagues. Instead of arguing over the data, they ought to be defining their presuppositions.

The real contribution of the transpersonal psychologist at this point has been the emphasis on the larger world of the spiritual element in man. Man's yearnings for transcendence have been evident throughout all of his history and should be the subject of study. A second contribution is that the transpersonal psychologist has been willing to venture into the data of unexplained, paranormal phenomena. A world view needs to explain *all* of the data if it is to be considered true and not just a working model. Naturalistic and humanistic psychologies have not embraced the whole of human nature.

Transpersonal psychologists, though, have not given a convincing argument as to why their experience of reality is to be accepted as true over any other spiritual world view such as that of Judaism, Christianity, or the Muslim faith.

*The built-in trouble with all these existential expe-
riences is that the content of such an experience is
not open to communication. Only the unknowing
would demand, "Please describe to me in normal
categories what you have experienced."*

Francis Schaeffer

TRANSPERSONAL
EXPERIENCE
AND TRUTH

In evaluating the transpersonal world view, we must realize how radical a departure it is from our usual ways of looking at reality. Our major concern at this point ought to be the question of epistemology, or how we know or learn about reality. Remember that we investigated problems with the method of knowing in naturalistic psychology. The exponents of that world view say that what is measurable and repeatable under experimental conditions is the true reality. However, this statement eliminates a genuine area of truth concerning human nature. A strict empiricist cannot "know" about the human mind and inner experience, nor about any nonphysical beings in the universe.

Therefore, we need to expand this naturalistic epistemology to learn more about man. However, transpersonal psychologists have not really expanded the empirical way of knowing but have substituted human experience for human reason as the new knowledge base. When experience is thus elevated, rationality is always lost.

Those holding the transpersonal world view say that the personal, inner experience in an altered state of consciousness is the definition of what is true and real. We must be careful not to deny such experience as a source of knowledge. In daily living we might give a piece of fried chicken to a friend and say, "Taste this and see for yourself how good it is." Even in the scientific enterprise we must experience the readings on our laboratory instruments in order to know.

However, the advocates of the transpersonal world view have made altered conscious experience the highest definition of truth and reality. This is done when the transpersonal thinker says that the universe is a unity with himself because he has experienced a loss of self and so has entered the cosmic consciousness during his meditation or drug taking. But in affirming the inner reality, he ends up denying our ordinary, daily experience of the world. How can it be said that the altered consciousness and its experience of egoless existence are more true than one's daily experience of individual personality? The transpersonal psychologist points to the research on subatomic particles as supporting the Eastern view of reality. But why should our observations (scientific experiences) in physics be trusted? We did not have scientific experiences during drug trips, meditation, or other altered states of awareness.

What has been said may not be a true test of the worth of an epistemology, but we do note that even transpersonal psychologists live as if regular consciousness, not altered conscious experience, is the source of truth. They teach one epistemology and yet live another. A person who sets up altered experience as truth should not worry about conforming himself to the reality of the physical world or any of its consequences. This is because the transpersonal scientist would say that one cannot ever know the real, physical world behind his sense experience. Many say that a physical world is not a real basis for experience at all. Reality takes the form of perceptual experiences in one's mind. A dream world is as real as your sitting in a chair reading this book. Your mind-brain creates each experience and shapes what you see because of your expectations, culture, and language. Our real question is, Is there a real world beyond one's sensory experience? The interesting fact is that the transpersonal thinker, whether he is an Eastern monk or a weekend meditator, lives as if there is such a real world behind experience.

If someone poured hot tea on a transpersonal

psychologist, he would probably jump just like the rest of us. But if he were true to his epistemology, what should he do? He should realize that the hot tea coming his way is just an experience (not really hot tea). If this is true, he should, therefore, be able to create his own inner experience (reality) and not notice (not be hurt by) the hot tea.

I admit that the mind can affect our perception of hot tea or a dentist's drill, but the real question is, Is the tea really there? Many an Eastern yogi, as well as persons under hypnosis, have used mental control over autonomic, nervous system responses that control the perception of pain, as well as bleeding or blistering on the body surface. But such control of the perception of pain—or a mystic not sensing the tea at all—does not mean that it is not there.

The way to demonstrate the real world's presence in spite of private experience to the contrary is to increase the size of the reality we wish the mystic to think away. Let us use New York City traffic as an example. Any transpersonal thinker, even in the height of an altered state of consciousness, could not alter very much the experience he would have of stepping in front of a moving bus. Why couldn't he? If the world that the Westerner sees, with its buses and traffic, is not the real world but a product of his symbol system and cultural conditioning, why is it so easy for everyone to see and feel the impact of a bus after little training by our culture and so difficult (yes, even impossible) with a lifetime of training in meditating to ever remove the reality of this experience? Is it possible that the bus is real and that one's experience is only as accurate as it conforms to the real world?

The transpersonal psychologist lives as if the world is real. He walks on ground, opens doors, eats food, swats flies, and teaches his point of view. All of these acts are an acknowledgment of the real, though distorted, world that we see in our normal, conscious state. A meditator in a deep trance can be hit by a bus and die, even though he is experiencing another reality where there are no buses.

Why is it that we keep coming back to this world of normal consciousness? Why do we all have roughly the same picture of reality down through the ages, in all cultures, in all languages? The differences in picturing reality are minimal. We are born in this world that we all experience. We dream and then wake up here. We take LSD and "crash" here. People report seeing our motionless bodies in the corner of the room while we are experiencing flying to Mars during a drug trip.

I maintain that experience, while revealing something of reality, is not a creator of individualized reality. To deny the real world behind our everyday experience, however distorted our perception of it, is to leave ourselves on a sea of nihilistic nausea.

However, I would not be able to convince a transpersonal believer with these words (or even with the bus) because the issue is not one we can broach with logic or can test; the issue is rather a matter of basic assumptions. Real communication between a naturalist and a committed transpersonalist is not possible. Says philosopher Francis Schaeffer about experience being the essence of truth:

> The built-in trouble with all these existential experiences is that the content of such an experience is not open to communication. Only the unknowing would demand, "Please describe to me in normal categories what you have experienced."[1]

The same point is made by James Sire in *The Universe Next Door:*

TRANSPERSONAL EXPERIENCE AND TRUTH

We are caught in an impasse. The issue is primary: Either the self is god and the new consciousness is a readout of the implications of that, or the self is not god and thus is subject to the existence of things other than itself.

To the self that opts for its own godhead, there is no argument. The naturalist's charge that this is megalomania or the theist's accusation that it is blasphemy is beside the point. Theoretically such a self accepts as real only what it decides to accept. To pour a pot of hot tea on his head would be futile for a person convinced of his own deity.

Perhaps (but how can we know?) this is the situation of psychotics who have totally withdrawn from conversation with others. Are they making their own universe? What is their subjective state? Only if they awaken may we find out, and then memory is often dim if present at all. Their reports may be quite useless. If they awaken, they waken into our universe of discourse. But perhaps this universe is our made-up universe and we ourselves are alone in a corner of a hospital ward unwittingly dreaming we are reading this book which actually we have made up by our unconscious reality-projecting machinery.[2]

A fascinating example of the confusion in reality due to a transpersonal view of things is in "The Yellow Pill," a short, science-fiction story.[3] A psychotic "patient" and his "psychiatrist" have two separate experiences of reality. The "patient" thinks he is on board a spaceship and has killed some invading Venusian lizards, whereas his buddy, who imagines he is a psychiatrist, has just caught space madness and has tied the "patient" up. The "psychiatrist" believes he is a world-famous psychiatrist interviewing a homicidal maniac in a straitjacket who has just shot five people, claiming they were Venusian lizards. Neither man shows any signs of mental illness except from the other's view of reality. At the end of the story the "psychiatrist," doubting his own world, takes a yellow pill that helps increase perceptions of the real world. He then wakes up on a spaceship with dead Venusian lizards all around him. Embracing the transpersonal method of knowing by experience makes our present reality just as unreal as the foregoing experience. How do you know that one yellow pill later you won't wake up in a spaceship or a mental ward? The transpersonal thinker can never be sure.

If after you have read the above section you are still convinced that experience is the source of truth and reality, there is no point in reading the rest of the book, or any other book for that matter. I will raise arguments, not from a strictly naturalistic view but certainly from one in which it is believed there is a real world beyond the senses. To anyone who doesn't believe in the real world "out there," no amount of scientific, "worldly" data can convert him. Again, we see that the real intellectual battles in life are battles of beliefs and world views, not of scientific data. And so I must challenge you again and again to evaluate the reasons why you hold a particular world view. What is your basis of belief? If you are an experiential, transpersonal epistemologist, what is the basis for that belief?

A related phenomenon, which transpersonal adherents must explain, is the question of why experiences that expand consciousness are not limited to the awareness of an empty, personless, oneness reality. There are spiritual experiences, both in normal and in altered states of mind, that do not fit the cosmic picture of the East.

Many times the altered-consciousness state involves the awareness of beings with individual existence and personality. Personality should fade away as the oneness of all reality becomes apparent, but anthropologist Carlos Castaneda, rugged pioneer of the new consciousness, discovers beings during mescaline trips (and later without drugs), many of whom are extremely terrifying.[4] TM meditators report the presence of beings during deep meditation. Parapsychology does not hide its study of ghosts nor does it deny the presence of spirits as explanations for poltergeists and for communication during séances.

Dr. Raymond Moody, in his book *Life After Life,* catalogs the altered-consciousness states reported by individuals who have "died" and have been resuscitated.[5] Such persons do report out-of-body travel and a feeling of oneness with reality, but they also report a continued conscious identity and the meeting of the spirits of angels or of departed loved ones. So it seems as if the new dimension revealed by altered states of awareness may not really be a great, unknowing, cosmic consciousness after all. Such experiences as these must be included in the transpersonal world view. Actually, much of the transpersonal experience may be better explained by the traditional Christian view of occult demons and powers. What occurs in the transpersonal experiences and contacts with other beings is not always blissful and glorious. It can be terrifying, cruel, and perverse. There are not always enlightened beings waiting on the other side, but by the admission of some transpersonalists sometimes fallen angels are there waiting.

Christian mystics, quite experienced in methods used to reach the altered-consciousness experience, interpret these experiences, not as viewing the essence of reality, but as viewing the inner mind void of distracting thoughts. The bliss associated with such viewing arises from the fact that what is being observed and experienced is the image of God (not God) in man. This image is not their goal but only the method used to withdraw from the world in order to meditate more consciously on the personal God of the Bible. Again, one's interpretation of the experience depends on one's world view. J. Stafford Wright supports this thesis in his *Mind, Man and the Spirits:*

> The interpretation of the experience largely rests upon the presuppositions of the mystic. If the mystic has no belief in God, the experience will be interpreted non-theologically. . . .[6]

The transpersonal thinker is caught in an example of circular reasoning. His experience creates his presuppositions, but he interprets all of his experience in the light of his presuppositions. World-view presuppositions, even those of the Christian who sees occult phenomena and a personal God as he looks at transpersonal experiences, can be rationally defended on grounds other than experience. The transpersonal world-view adherents, on the other hand, are disqualified by their own epistemology, and thus they cannot explain many transpersonal phenomena.

EXPLANING (AWAY) HUMAN NATURE

Transpersonal psychology still leaves unexplained the phenomenon of the human. Transpersonal psychology shares with naturalistic and humanistic psychologies the belief in a closed universe—a universe not open to any creative act from the outside. Everything within the universe has to be explained by the universe itself. The problem then becomes one of explaining man's consciousness and transcendence over nature.

Some of the more physically minded transpersonal thinkers suggest that every part of nature partakes in the reality of mind and consciousness.

Those who hold this view believe that the subatomic particles themselves are elementary bits of both matter and mind, depending on the way we choose to look at them. In quantum physics, the principle of complementarity ascribes to subatomic entities a dual nature—the capacity to behave both as a particle and as a wave of nonmatter. The view then is that combinations of such particles produce the world as we see it, including self-conscious minds. The Jesuit philosopher-biologist Teilhard de Chardin made popular such a view in his *Phenomenon of Man*. He suggested a grand, evolutionary scheme in which conscious atoms evolved into man and in which man was evolving toward total consciousness, or the *noösphere*—a term he coined. Sir Julian Huxley, in the introduction to this book, wrote, "*The Phenomenon of Man* has affected a threefold synthesis—of the material and physical world with the world of mind and spirit; of the past with the future; and of variety with unity, the many with the one."[7]

This view depends on two ideas for which we have no verifiable data—only assumption: (1) We have never observed, nor are we likely to observe, any level of consciousness in atomic particles. Because of the privacy of experience it is impossible even to prove empirically that animals are conscious. We assume some of them are because of their complicated reactive and proactive behavior patterns. These behaviors are similar to our own consciously generated behaviors and allow us to assume there is consciousness in higher animals. Physical particles, on the other hand, demonstrate only loosely determined motion. Maybe it is unfair to ask of an atom what a person demonstrates, but I am doing this only to reveal that this view is based on assumption. World view, not data, has produced this view.

(2) The gestalt view, that combinations of matter cause new properties to emerge in the whole that are not present in its parts, is also without data support. In this case putting together atoms that supposedly have a "glimmer" of consciousness produces a self-conscious man. This phenomenon cannot be demonstrated by putting atoms together to see if a human results. (Remember, Frankenstein was only science fiction!) Such gestalt thinking depends on clinging to a world view without a creative God. Says one scientist about Teilhard de Chardin and this view of the whole's being greater than the sum of its parts:

> Teilhard de Chardin, following Leibniz, weaves an ingeniously poetic but unconvincing construct of conscious atoms. Man can be conscious because his atoms and molecules and cells are crudely conscious. Such a scheme need fail because atomic consciousness avails naught without a mechanism for integrating the little primitive bits of consciousness into the sublime entity of experience which all men possess. [8]

This raising of the similarity between the world view of particle physics and the mystic is an attempt to explain man and mind, or the discontinuity between man and matter, by raising all nature to the level of mind and spirit. [9] This is the same method, but the opposite approach, used by the naturalistic psychologist, who does away with the discontinuity between man and nature by denying the mind and by lowering man to the level of nature. However, the real issue on the nature of man is *explaining* the discontinuity between man and nature, not *explaining it away.* We must admit to the force of our daily observations about the uniqueness of man within the world of nature. Man is alive, conscious, self-conscious, creative, communicative, and a culture builder. He towers above everything else in nature, and all of our psychology tells us that. Practicing a psychology that emphasizes only one percent of the data—the similarity of chimps to people, or people to atoms—is a shallow psychology. The purpose in such a limiting psychology is to destroy the discontinuity we find between people and nature, and thus not have to explain human nature. Many a world view will fall if it has to explain the phenomenon of man.

This is the path taken by the transpersonal psychologist. Yes, there may be nonphysical properties of matter, but the leap from that belief to man as we see him is enormous. Only the pressure of a world view could allow psychologists to compare the conscious life of man to the unknown state of an atom.

Therefore, we cannot make the jump of the behaviorist and say with B. F. Skinner that inner experience is only an illusion, or of the mystic and say with him that atoms and trees are essentially just like man. The only way such statements can be made is by embracing a world view that does not allow for our most successful method of observing man. The naturalist says no to nonempirical observations. Therefore, he finds man to be a rock and a monkey. The transpersonal psychologist says that the unity experience is reality—that all is one. Therefore, atoms, rocks, and stars are all conscious. However, in all this world-view reshuffling, man as we observe him is left unexplained.

EXPERIENCE:
REAL SOLUTIONS VERSUS FADS

A criticism in the area of solutions to problems can be leveled against all technological and spiritual claims to solutions of human problems. However, few systems of thought have produced such meager results as the transpersonal world view has. It has not produced the new man nor workable solutions to problems such as mental illness, social unrest, or war. And it has all the appearances of being a big "rip-off."

An article in *Psychology Today* described the problems of applying the transpersonal world view to real life:

> It is difficult for the romantic imagination to work, to decide, to recognize the value of conflict and anger, to get tough, to be efficient, to deal with the reality of evil and the fact of human suffering. Strategies for the use of power, plans for social change, working within institutions and relationships with known limits are all difficult.
>
> It is easy to flow, to go with it, to travel in the far-out spaces of the mind and the emotions but it is difficult to make commitments, accept discipline, recognize limits, and become an individuated, responsible self.[10]

This is not to say that spiritual reality does not exist and that man does not need to be a part of it, but as we look at thousands of years in the Eastern world, the cosmic experiences have not changed the essential character of human problems and anguish. The West has its share of problems, but at least those who have naturalistic, humanistic, and theistic approaches sit down and design therapies that fit mental illnesses and work out educational, political, or business technologies for change. In the East and its transpersonal thought, men withdraw and talk of enlightenment, and yet very little light is shed on ways to save humanity. Harvey Cox, on the faculty of the Harvard Divinity School, made a thorough analysis of the American interest in the Eastern ways of thinking as an answer to problems. He said:

TRANSPERSONAL EXPERIENCE AND TRUTH

What the Easterners are doing is hardly a prescription for a general cure; rather it is a symptom of a malaise with which we all must contend. Religious remedies to the ills of a culture take two basic forms: one tries to get at the underlying causes of the malady; the other provides a way for people to live in spite of the illness, usually by providing them with an alternative mini world, sufficiently removed from the outside so that its perils are kept away from the gate. The Easterners have almost all chosen this second form. The only solution they offer to other people is to join them in their mini world.

But if we all join them, it would soon be a maxi world with all the problems back again.[11]

Here in this country we also see the popularization of transpersonal experience for those who can pay. We have TM schools, the dancing of Sufi meditation, the baths of the Esalen Institute, the toilet training and irrelevant lectures of est (Erhard Seminars Training), Silva Mind Control, exercise and meditation at the Arica Institute, biofeedback machines, bioenergetic techniques, the pain of Rolfing—a deep muscle massage—karate and aikido, Zen tennis, Zen football, the Theosophical Society, the Rosicrucian Fellowship, yoga exercise, Maharaj-Ji and the Divine Light Mission, The International Society for Krishna Consciousness, astrology, I Ching interpretations, biorhythm analysis, psychic healing, ad nauseam.[12] It all begins to sound like wealthy Americans discovering the latest fad and experience, not a change of person or of view, only a painless search for spiritual experience and not spiritual truth.

Psychiatrist Perry London once described the motivation behind psychotherapies in the West. The time of Freud was a period of sexual prohibition, and therefore a therapy of subconscious and sexual analysis arose to meet the need. Then in the years after World War II everyone had anxiety, and therapies arose to attack anxiety. Now in the 70s we are in the Age of Ennui, or boredom, and these transpersonal experiences are our therapy. Truth? Who cares? Experience? Bring it on![13]

Let us admit, though, that the world is real, and so are its problems. It will take correct steps in personal and social living and in the entering into true, spiritual enlightenment to produce a healthy, happier world.

Only when the hope of harmonizing theory with reality is abandoned does an ideological revolution occur.

Frank Severin

INADEQUATE PSYCHOLOGICAL WORLD VIEWS

It seems as if the naturalistic, humanistic, and transpersonal world views fail to cover adequately all the data we find on human nature. Let us recall what a world view is. It is a framework of truth, not just a big working model. It is as close to truth as possible. It cannot be just a convenient theory for experimentation purposes. It has to be the truth, the whole truth, and nothing but the truth. The advocates of all three psychological world views we have analyzed spoke to only part of the data in psychology, but no view was "large enough" so that all the data could be explained. Therefore, none of the views should qualify as our world view in psychology. The fact that people persist in keeping these views as belief systems seems to arise from their unreasonable clinging to key assumptions, even in the face of contradictory data on human nature.

PUZZLE BUILDING

Imagine, if you will, that we have a giant, one-thousand-piece puzzle. Someone dumps it on the floor before us and tells us to put it together. How do we begin? Most people begin with the edges because they are straight and because the completed puzzle usually has four straight sides. This is the key idea in searching for truth, as well as in puzzle building. We need to know something about the final product before we can meaningfully begin putting the puzzle together.

What if you picked up a piece of blue from the pile of puzzle pieces? Where does the piece go? You look at the picture on the box top; let's say it is a picture of Niagara Falls. The box top shows you that the ultimate picture will have a blue sky and white water. Therefore, the blue piece in your hand must belong in the sky somewhere. The box top is like a world view. It is like a picture into which all the particular facts in the world must eventually fit.

How does our naturalistic psychologist put together the puzzle on man? Some naturalists say that the puzzle did not come with a box-top picture. We must put the pieces together and see what picture of reality emerges. But there is a problem in doing that. There are too many pieces, too many facts on the human to handle. Since knowledge is doubling approximately every seven years, there will be eight times as many facts available on man in twenty-one years as there are today. It is just as if when you get one hundred pieces of the puzzle together, someone comes into the room and dumps out two hundred more pieces. You will never finish, and in fact your job keeps getting bigger. This is the problem with naturalistic science today. Every year our introductory textbooks in science get larger because there are more facts available than previously. But facts alone cannot create our picture on man. Facts on the biology of pregnancy, for example, will not tell a woman if she should have an abortion or not.

The naturalist, though, does put together many of the pieces on the biology of man. However, when he gets pieces showing mind or spirit in man, he rebels against this as being unscientific. He ignores the pieces because he believes they come from some theologian's antiquated puzzle and are not part of the true picture of human nature.

The humanistic psychologist is quick to pick up the pieces that the naturalistic psychologist dropped, but he, too, makes mistakes. He says that we cannot ignore the pieces on the human mind and experience but goes on to ignore those pieces that deal with God, the source of the human's uniqueness. The humanistic psychologist also ignores those pieces that deal with fallen human nature. This psychologist has a box-top picture in mind, and he is going to make the pieces fit.

We see a relativism creeping into the humanistic psychologist's puzzle building as he decides that everyone can make any picture he wants with the pieces on man's problems and purposes. There is no absolute picture for the human being. Yes, the pieces for biology are true and fit as a boundary for the picture. But no, we will make our own picture for man's life style. The humanistic psychologist even takes scissors and cuts many of the pieces to make them fit his puzzle. He admits to absolute truth in biology and physics because when he is ill, he wants the doctor to use "facts" to cure him. But the humanistic thinker says that there are no absolute rules that govern human relationships and ways of living.

Finally, the transpersonal psychologist picks up the puzzle and says, "You have misunderstood all the rules for puzzle building. The pieces don't have to fit together; in fact, 'nonfit' is the only rule. You can bunch some of them up here and some there. Red does not always have to border red; be creative." Of course, those with such thinking can produce any picture that is a part of their feelings for the moment. The fact that all the pieces on man appear to fit one way is only due to our distorted perceptions.

The point that I am making is, Is there a truth about reality and man? Is there a box-top picture that we can count on? If truth is all but lost to the determinism of the naturalist and the experiential relativism of the humanist and transpersonalist, why even take the time to investigate data? Our world view does not have to be complete or inflexible, but we should have confidence that it points to reality. The naturalistic, humanistic, and transpersonal world views do not inspire such confidence. They avoid obvious data on human nature and leave our puzzle unfinished. Let me summarize the inadequacies that we have seen thus far in these three psychological world views.

INADEQUATE SOURCE FOR MAN'S ESSENCE

Philosopher Francis Schaeffer coined the term *mannishness* to describe all the characteristics of man that distinguish him from the animal world. These are his self-conscious mind and rationality, personality, moral notions, creativity, true language usage, and religious aspirations.

Psychology's basis for all that man is, is either the materialism of the naturalist or the panpsychism of the transpersonalist. The materialist says that matter and energy + time + chance is the basis for what we see in man. The adherent of panpsychism accepts some of the "mannishness" in man but presents as its source the personality present in all matter. Our best evidence supports neither of these two views. Psychologists who insist on holding either of these views spend their time bending over backwards to deny the personality and mind of man or to find personality and minds in atoms.

In all of these psychological world views the basis for man is found in nature. And questions remain unanswered. How do we get personality out of a rock? How do we explain such things as the aspirations, loves, creativity, communication, spiritual longings of man? To deny man or to elevate nature is no answer. Francis Schaeffer declares:

> No one has presented an idea, let alone demonstrated it to be feasible, to explain how the impersonal beginning, plus time, plus chance, can give personality. We are distracted by

INADEQUATE PSYCHOLOGICAL WORLD VIEWS

a flourish of endless words, and lo, personality has appeared out of the hat! This is water rising above its source. No one in all the history of humanistic, rationalistic thought has found a solution. As a result, either the thinker must say man is dead, because personality is a mirage; or else he must hang his reason on a hook outside the door and cross the threshold into the leap of faith which is the new level of despair.[1]

What we need is a Personality behind the personality of man in order to explain his essence.

INADEQUATE EXPLANATION OF MAN'S CHARACTER FLAW

For all time and in all disciplines thinkers have seen man's irrationality. We call it his inhumanity, and yet it is very much human. Lack of education will not explain it. Educated man has not lost his inhumanity. Bad environment will not explain it. All environments, including the rich, beautiful, religious, reinforcing, and unreinforcing produce their share of human weakness. Pointing to incomplete evolution will not explain it. Animals do not suffer the same behavioral irrationality as man. To believe they are evolved beyond man is not thinkable. Brain problems cannot explain it. Men with no observable abnormalities commit most of the "crimes" of life. Most people with physical abnormalities are not the major criminals of society. All people admit to the difficulty of doing what they know is right and actually wish to do. What can possibly explain this major observation about people?

We must not overlook it in our psychology, since solutions to mental illness, interpersonal conflict, and social problems are some of our primary concerns. There is a growing tendency in psychology, though, to solve the problem of man's character flaw by redefining it. If enough people suffer from the problem, it is normal and no longer a problem. We see an emphasis on the "normalness" of aggressive, selfish behavior from geneticists and sociobiologists. It is only one's genes looking out for his or her own future. In humanistic and transpersonal psychology, despite Maslow's goal of the self-actualized, perfect human, we see that the emphasis on moral relativism is destroying any labeling of categories of good or bad in behavior. Once these categories are lost, the strivings for changing people's "sin" nature disappear in psychology. However, relabeling behavior in human nature is not explanation enough. What we need in psychology is an explanation for the reason every human has a flaw in his innermost being and what is the nature of this flaw.

INADEQUATE EXPLANATION FOR MAN'S SPIRITUAL NATURE

The naturalistic psychologist has too long ignored the spiritual side of man's nature. Man, unlike any animal, looks beyond the physical world and strives for meaning and completeness in this life and even beyond. He has always worshiped and has been aware of spiritual reality. Those who develop psychologies of religion to explain away people's transcending urges should consider the very real probability that the spiritual world exists and that they are meant to be a part of it. This spiritual nature and longing in man needs to be studied. There are no naturalistic humans in battlefield foxholes, only naturalistic theories.

The transpersonal explanation for the spiritual nature of man is his essential oneness with the universe. However, denying the reality or importance of individual personality is an "antipsychology." This is difficult to call a true psychology, since individual personality is the major reality we observe in psychology. We occasionally dream or we feel one with nature on a Colorado backpacking trip, but we live our lives as individuals, within the boundaries of self. We need a theory of spirituality that will admit to the reality of self-existence and its needs. No solutions to man's spiritual longings will be found until he looks in the right direction. The transpersonal model has not produced the change in people toward a supposed oneness existence; enlightenment has not come, and we begin to expect that self is here to stay. What is needed in psychology is a true picture of man's spiritual nature and need.

INADEQUATE EPISTEMOLOGY TO STUDY THE WHOLE PERSON

Carl Rogers, in an article entitled "Some Questions and Challenges Facing a Humanistic Psychology," wrote:

> We are not fond of a mechanistically oriented, hard-headed empiricism. But what will we put in its place? An existential mysticism will not in my judgement, be good enough. Private subjective opinion will not be good enough. What is to be our way of knowing, of adding to knowledge?[2]

This statement by Rogers accurately reflects the dilemma of modern psychology in the study of human nature. On the one hand, we can choose a strict empiricism and learn much about man's body and behavior but lose sight of the inner person. On the other hand, we can study our own experience and the privacy of our inner nature, directly, but we can in no way be guaranteed that our private experience corresponds to reality.

This dilemma becomes extremely important as we construct our world-view assumptions about human nature. As we have seen, one's world-view assumptions about man color the way one interprets scientific data and personal experience. How, then, can we use a smattering of biological data or experience to construct our world view? This using-world-view-to-interpret-data-to-build-world-view can be nothing other than a circular trap of proving what one already believes. What is needed is another source of knowledge about those areas of human nature that are beyond the realm of science or experience. There is reason to assume that the finite human with finite reason cannot reach for all the data potentially within his grasp and sufficiently understand his own nature.

The naturalistic denial of that in the human beyond the physical and the humanistic and transpersonal denial of any absolute truth about human nature remove the epistemological problems of the three world-view adherents. However, this is explaining away, not explaining, a difficult problem.

INADEQUATE GUIDELINES FOR SOLUTIONS

Finally, as psychologists press for solutions to people's problems, they have a need for true, ethical guidelines. That is, there must be a basis for deciding what is good or not good, helpful or harmful, right or wrong in our approach to solving human problems. To say that good is that which contributes to the development of the optimum or the self-actualized state does not remove the need for a reference definition of what exactly an optimum personality is. One can answer that he has picked certain arbitrary qualities that he feels are part of optimum human mental health. But there is a problem here. Someone else can, with equal sincerity, pick different, even opposite qualities.

What the majority of psychologists feel is an optimum personality or life style (sociological majority); what the normal personality is or does (statistical optimum); and the approval of any personality type or life style as "all right" (moral relativism) are all arbitrary evaluations to guide us in our work. Do these evaluations really tell us, for example, if conformity is a virtue or a vice? Or since premarital chastity is rare, must someone who practices it be considered personally abnormal? Is homosexuality an illness? How about sex with animals?

The point is, How do you decide such questions without absolute reference points as to man's nature, life style, and purpose? To deny that such absolutes in ethics and morality exist is to do so by presupposition and is to leave psychology directionless. Someone may claim that an absolute does not exist, but he or she cannot claim that there isn't a need for absolute reference points on human nature.

In summary, we need a world view to encompass all the data we find in psychology. We need to explain the origin and nature of physical, mental, and spiritual dimensions of man, as well as human nobility (mannishness) and irrationality (fallenness). An immaterial, personal, intelligent, creative, eternal agency is needed behind the origins of all that man is. And we need, and are hopelessly lost without, an absolute, communicated picture of truth to guide us in our method of knowing and our search for ethical guidelines. All of these are issues in psychology and enter into all psychological discussions of human life and happiness.

What world view can we use to guide a complete study of human nature? The next chapter explores one—Christian theism.

The believer in Christian theism holds to a personal, communicative creator God as the source of man's essence and personality. The Christian theist also regards the historic fall of the human race as integral to understanding people's moral, intellectual, and emotional problems. Let us briefly examine this world view.

THE MAJOR COMPONENTS OF A CHRISTIAN THEISM WORLD VIEW

The Nature of Reality

The Christian theist says that the universe contains both material and immaterial reality. There exists a God who is a spirit person, eternal, transcendent (beyond nature), and immanent (present everywhere). This God became a human and communicated with humans in the person of Jesus Christ. This God is the creative source of all the universe and its order, of life, and of personality. The universe, then, is not a fatalistic machine but is open to the actions and influence of God.

In such a universe man can discover truth in three ways. These three should be considered a hierarchy of knowledge in terms of their dependability and scope. Our highest source of truth is divine revelation. This is God's speaking to men and women in the Bible and through the person of Jesus Christ about reality. However, this revelation is not exhaustive truth. We can also learn by experiment in the scientific method because the physical universe follows laws of cause and effect and our minds are capable of understanding much of the order in reality. Experience is also a source of truth for man but is third in the hierarchy. We are conscious beings and can "touch" reality in our experience. Such human experience needs the guidance of logic and rationality, and both experience and experiment need the overall framework of revelation.

The nature of certain spiritual truth about man is fully available only in revelation, since through experiment and experience people are limited in what they can investigate. The scientist cannot study people's spiritual nature or needs, or the nature of any other spiritual beings in the universe. He cannot study any event of importance to human nature such as the Creation or the Fall, since history is beyond replication in laboratories. Unaided by revelation, the scientist must assume that in the past human nature was in the same basic form that we observe in the present.

Through experience we can tell that spiritual reality is there, but we cannot interpret its nature, meaning, and the reasons people do not normally partake in it. Neither science nor experience can reveal the future of man and what lies beyond the grave.

All the answers to these questions, however, can be told to us by someone who knows the answers. And it is the Christian theist's claim, that God has revealed such knowledge to man. This is only a claim, but what is important is that the truth of this claim is open to investigation. If the Bible is revelation from God to people, it certainly is the most important source of truth available to us.

Christians, including Christian psychologists, trust the Bible to be revelation from God because it makes sense both to their reasoning and to their experiences. One can investigate revelation because it is written down. The Bible seems to be very accurate in its account of ancient history, contains descriptions of nature in harmony with reason and science, fits the nature of human problems, has passed through history virtually unchanged, contains hundreds of marvelously fulfilled prophecies, and has very reasonable answers to the common objections to Christianity. The Bible's central character is Jesus Christ, a person of history who claimed deity, worked miracles, and rose from the grave.[1] Generations of Christians, of all races and backgrounds, have given force to the truth of these claims. Finally, the personal experience of the Christian, after he has aligned his mind, heart, and will to the God of the Bible, helps to confirm the truth of these beliefs.

If anyone feels, after investigating these evidences, that they are not sufficient as a basis for belief in the validity and reliability of the Bible and the teachings of Christ, I must ask, "Is the data insufficient, or does your current, nontheistic world view cause you to set such a high threshold on evidences for miracles, Deity, resurrections, etc., that no reasonable amount of data could ever change your mind?" If the latter is the case, you must allow Christian theism to compete on the same footing with your own world view. Does your world view have as much evidence as Christian theism has to support it? If not, why do you still hold to it? I have never met a person who was willing to investigate the evidences behind Christian theism and then, whether he embraced Christianity or not, did not admit that in Christianity are presented strong evidences worth considering.

The major problem with those holding the other psychological world views today is that they have gone out of their way to avoid the obvious need for a personal, creative origin for the world and man. Matter did not just happen. Man is not a machine. There is no scientific data against the assumption of a personal, creative God being behind the nature of man. There could be no such scientific data, since scientists cannot study spirits or historical events. All that psychologists can do is to put forward counter assumptions such as materialism or panpsychism, through which the data we have collected on man are twisted and distorted. A personal, creative God gives man a beginning, a future, and meaning and purpose in his present existence.

The Nature of Man

Man is seen as a "half-breed" creature in Christian theism, capable of participation in both material and immaterial realities. The Bible says that man is a unity of matter and spirit. Genesis 2:7 declares, "And the Lord God formed man of the dust of the ground, and breathed into his nostrils the breath of life; and man became a living soul." Therefore, man is *composed of* matter and spirit, but he *is* a soul—something different from either matter or spirit. This is in good agreement with neurophysiological studies that demonstrate an almost inseparable relationship between brain and mind in man. *Monism* probably is the term that best fits the nature of man; but it is not the materialistic monism of the naturalist nor the pantheistic monism of the transpersonalist. It should be called "Hebraic monism" because of its description in the Old Testament.

Man is also a trichotomous being in that he is capable of, and needing to, participate in three levels of life. He must relate to matter according to its laws (eat, drink, sleep), to other individuals socially, and to God in true, spiritual ways.

Man does have a body as described by the naturalistic psychologist, and there are rules to describe his conscious and unconscious processes. This by no means implies that man is a determined creature, only that some of his behaviors are predictable when the major influences on him are known.

Man is also more than body in that he has a self-conscious mind, a result of the creative act of God. He is shown to be more than animal because of this creative act and because of the special capacities of the human mind. This does not deny that animals have minds and are intelligent, but it does deny that they have the capacities of man to relate personally and morally with human beings and with God. Man is a lofty, creative, communicative, personal being because of these capacities to relate.

Man also has spiritual needs and capacities. The Bible explains the human being's spiritual nature in terms of his being created in the image of God (Genesis 1:26,27), meaning that he was created to share in the very life of God and to be a "house" for the living God. This is an astounding truth. Men and women were made with personality, creativity, morality, and communicative skills to better reflect the nature of the spiritual God, who was to indwell them. Man is made in God's image in somewhat the same way that a glove is made in the image of a hand so as to unite with a hand that gives it movement and body. The human, however, is not just a material "glove" for God but personally alive and self-conscious and meant to have the spiritual God revealed in part through his essence and behavior. This is spiritual life and makes men and women eternal creatures of true worth.

Man Is Fallen

At birth humans are capable of relating to only a portion of reality. Because of the historic fall of Adam and Eve, every person lost his spiritual relationship with God but not the need for this relationship. Each human inherits this loss in much the same way that a baby, whose parents are exiled from their homeland, is born without the citizenship they had enjoyed. In spite of the Fall, we can still see man's goodness and noble image. Because of the Fall, though, we have an explanation for his dissatisfaction and lack of fulfillment in life, his self-centeredness, and his spiritual longings. Let me say this again. The main effect of the Fall on the psychology of man is that he is the center of his own life, the source of his own unhappiness, and is inadequate in himself to meet his deepest needs. This is evidenced in the strength of his selfish desires, his weak self-image, his incessant guilt, and his difficulty in practicing altruism. The important point is that while this may be the way man is, it is not the way he was meant to be. And no psychology book can tell you that. Without these truths on the condition of man, our psychologies just try to beautify the fallen human nature and, at best, only manage to delay its inevitable decay.

Solutions to Man's Problems

Since every person is a being with needs and capacities in three dimensions of life, problems can arise in all three of these dimensional needs. Interrelationships among problems in these three are the rule. A Christian psychologist admits to the reality of physical and mental problems in human nature, and further admits that true solutions can be found in these areas. However, until men and women live as they were intended to, i.e., related to God and without self-centeredness, they will always be searching for real life. In their search they do what does not satisfy, they use people, they acquire true guilt, and they improperly ground their self-image—all of which adversely affect mental health.

The Christian gospel as taught by Jesus Christ provides the solution to these problems. Jesus died in man's place for his sin nature, and each one has the choice now to enter into spiritual relationship with God through Christ. God, then, joins with such a person's nature, replacing a self-centered existence with the God-centered one for which he was created. In Christianity, this new life is called the new birth. Make no mistake—a person can be changed from within, even though this is not immediately visible to our empirical eyesight.

God does not change much of the old life of a person in giving the new life. Old bodies and many old habits still remain, and we suffer decay in these areas, but a Christian is in the process of learning how spiritual life applies to such problems. The effects of the sin nature are still with even the most fervent of Christians, and perfection in body and mind is not possible in this life. However, Christians are continually renewing their minds and emotions in life in accordance with personal contact with God and spiritual life; thus, psychological methods can be used more effectively on them than on others. They have God at the center of their beings and after death receive new bodies free from the consequences of the Fall.

Those with solutions from a Christian-based psychology also enjoy the confidence of having absolute guidelines of truth in terms of values and morals with regard to human nature and behavior. A Christian psychologist has a basis for saying the individual person is more valuable than all of nature, for saying that adultery is not an acceptable practice, and for describing man's deepest needs. God, the architect of human nature, has spoken to us concerning these areas.

The following is a chart that summarizes the ways in which Christian theism fits the inadequacies we discovered in traditional psychological world views.

Psychology's Inadequacy	Christian Theism's Answer
1. There is no explanation for the origin of man's personhood.	There exists a personal, creator God.
2. There is no explanation for the evil drive within man and the inability to remain other-centered.	Man fell into sin and bears the consequences of a self-centered, spiritually dead existence.
3. There is no explanation for man's spiritual yearnings.	The spiritual world exists, and man has the capacity and need to relate to the God of the universe.
4. There is no adequate method of knowing about people's mental and spiritual nature and needs.	The God-inspired Bible reveals truth concerning the inner nature and ultimate needs of all people.
5. There are no absolute guidelines for applying solutions to people's problems. Ethical and moral discussions are beyond the scope of the scientific method.	Absolute truth is revealed by God concerning human nature, purpose, and life style.

A WORLD VIEW THAT MAKES A DIFFERENCE

Some might say at this point that it seems as if I have just added a little religion to psychology. But this is not the case. I have not discussed religion in this chapter but have discussed another world view. As we have seen, one's beliefs in a world view have a tremendous effect on an academic field of study.

Also, it might be said that the world view of Christian theism is not needed in psychology since there are many acceptable ways to get to the same truth about human nature. This statement, though, misses the point of how far awry a wrong world view can take one in his or her academic field. Psychology can be awry not only because of errors psychologists hold so that they can maintain inaccurate world views but also insofar as psychologists discover some true facts and applications but miss other facts with superior applications.

I have also heard it said that some academic fields are so empirically based that they are immune from the effects of world-view presuppositions. The same facts, it is argued, will be discovered no matter what the underlying beliefs of the scientist are. Fields such as math, biology, and medicine are the most often mentioned in this line of thought. How could a world view possibly affect the study of biology or of medicine? Actually it can and does. What happens is not necessarily that error arises in a scientific field because of an inadequate world view but that the *best* data and solutions in a field are never realized because of the biases that arise from a scientist's particular world view.

Biology does not have to be a scientific field, as in the Western world, in which we lay a dead animal on a table and dissect its inner parts. It is not that we don't know and discover truth in this way, but someone with a different world view might see animals less as machines and might rather study them as they live in ecological systems. One could also study the wisdom of God in the character traits of animal instincts.[2]

The emphasis in medicine can be either on its preventative or its therapeutic use, depending on one's world view, and the content of medical texts would change accordingly. Solutions to medical problems—whether they be surgery, drugs, diet, massage and posture techniques, counseling, or the casting out of evil spirits—depend on one's "slant" on life.

So, too, one's psychology varies greatly with world-view assumptions, and we should not expect a Christian psychology to be just a naturalistic or humanistic psychology with a few Bible verses thrown in. The world-view statements of Christian theism are detailed and far-reaching. It has been argued that any "Christian" academic approach will resemble that of Western science because the Western scientific tradition had its origins in the Christian world view. This is certainly true in some fields. However, we must remember that by the time psychology was born in the West, Western science had kicked away its Christian scaffolding and had embraced naturalism. In addition, today's Western psychology is perhaps more strongly influenced by modern, "liberal," Christian theology and the Eastern religions than by the traditional Christian world view. Therefore, we cannot depend on modern psychology to continue to parallel elements in the Christian world view, if indeed it does so now.

What, then, would Christian theists produce in the way of a study of human nature if they rigorously emphasized their beliefs? What would a Christian psychology be like, and how would it differ from psychology? I believe that the Christian world view would lead Christian psychologists to establish research and teaching priorities that might change the make-up of large areas of the present field.

First, I would expect Christian psychology to have more of an emphasis on preventative measures than on therapeutic ones to solve emotional and social problems. It seems as if the psychologists of our culture have largely developed therapeutic solutions. One reason for this might be the reluctance to suggest what are the right and the wrong principles in family and personal life that lead to psychological and sociological health or illness. It seems to be a general consensus in our culture that we are free to do what we like and that then we can use medicine and psychology to remove the consequences of our behavior. Adherents of a Christian psychology, I suggest, would seek to change the early influences that distort personality; make wide-sweeping changes in family and educational structures; and seek ways to integrate morality with modern life in ways that alleviate physical, emotional, and social problems.

Second, I believe a Christian psychology would be much more of an applied field than psychology now is. It seems as if the psychology books are filled with theories and data on such problems as mental illness, alcoholism, and crime, and yet these problems get worse every year. I do not think that psychological theories and approaches are necessarily wrong, but there doesn't seem to be the sustained interest, or funding, necessary to apply the theories to the problems of human beings until some relief is seen. Psychologists seem to lack the unity of purpose for serious, direct application and often seem more in love with collecting academic data than with the suffering people whom the data represent.

Third, I believe that those holding to a Christian

psychology would spend much time exploring several areas of biblical revelation about human nature, something not done in most secular psychologies. Christians believe that God, the creator of man, has unveiled much of the mystery in human nature, especially as it concerns man's spiritual nature. It is not that operant conditioning, for example, is unimportant or untrue as applied to man; but why should unconscious responses in man's body comprise such a huge amount of the interest, time, and money available to psychologists? If we believe that man is more than a machine—that he is spirit as well—we should then spend time and effort on this aspect of human nature proportional to its importance.

To study man's spiritual nature, Christian psychologists need first to develop an acceptable set of biblical hermeneutics, or method of biblical interpretation. We need to know what the boundaries of biblical academics are. What does the Bible teach about human psychology, and what is the method used to draw this biblical psychology from the pages of Scripture? Unfortunately, many Christian psychologists think that the Bible teaches only about God and salvation, and their psychology becomes indistinguishable from secular psychology. Included in the main message of the Bible about God, man, sin, and salvation are the nature and needs of humans before and after their regeneration by God. These are described in detail. We need to admit what the Bible itself claims—that it teaches much on the psychology of human nature.

With a well-though-out method of biblical interpretation, Christian psychologists need to spend much time in developing a biblical anthropology, or what the Bible teaches about human nature. The biblical study of man is not simple, and by no means are all Christians in agreement as to what it means.

Part of this biblical investigation needs to be a complete study of the spiritual nature of man. This investigation should include the severity of the Fall and in what ways it affected man's mind, emotions, and will. Also, a study of the ways to apply the principles of sanctification or growth in the spiritual dimension of life to people's psychological problems is needed. Many questions need to be answered. Are sanctification and mental health the same thing? How far should we go in our psychoengineering developments and the consequent reversing of the curses from God in Genesis 3? And many more.

CONCLUSION:
WORLD VIEWS IN COLLISION

As I close this book, I want to reemphasize the power of world views on our thinking. Academic thought is much more a product of belief systems than of data collection. In this sense all academic fields are "religious" at their bases. The real need, then, in academic thought, is to be aware of one's world-view assumptions. Once we know them, it is important to know the reasons we hold these beliefs. Have we just inherited them unthinkingly from our academic ancestors? And are they internally consistent? For example, does your view of origins agree with your description of man? And finally, do your assumptions fit the data that we find on man; i.e., does your world view fit the world you live in?

When viewed on this level, conflicts in academic thought can be seen to be not differences over the data but differences in underlying world views. The scholar who is aware of his world view and the reasons he holds it, who is aware of the world views of his academic adversaries, and who has a good grasp on the world of data is in a much better position to generate ideas and applications than if he were unaware of these things. If psychology has gone awry, it is because psychologists have ignored errors in their underlying belief systems, and because even when errors have been revealed, the psychologists have clung tenaciously to many assumptions that have no basis in logic or the factual world.

The Christian world view, by contrast, seems to be the best candidate for a world view on which to build a psychology. To argue that this is narrow-minded and biased against other religious beliefs is irrelevant, since our only question at this point ought to be, Is the Christian view of man and his problems defensible as truth? To argue for fairness to all religions is only denying that there could be "one truth," and this is an unsupported, world-view argument.

I feel that Christian theism offers the most defensible world view available to psychology. It fits our data and experience. It is broad enough to explain all the data on man, and yet it is detailed enough to be tested. If psychology is to develop and become effective in the lives of people, psychologists cannot continue to ignore the world view of Christian theism.

CHRISTIAN THEISM AND PSYCHOLOGY

1

¹Mark P. Cosgrove and James D. Mallory, Jr., *Mental Health: A Christian Approach* (Grand Rapids: Zondervan, 1977).

2

¹Gardner Murphy, *Historical Introduction to Modern Psychology* (New York: Harcourt, Brace and World, 1949), p. 13.

²Francis A. Schaeffer, *How Should We Then Live?* (Old Tappan, N.J.: Revell, 1976).

³Murphy, *Historical Introduction,* p. 116.

⁴Charles Darwin, *The Origin of Species, By Means of Natural Selection, Or the Preservation of Favored Races in the Struggle for Life* (New York and London: Merrill and Baker, 1859).

⁵Charles Darwin, *The Descent of Man, and Selection in Relation to Sex,* rev. ed. (New York and London: Merrill and Baker, 1874).

⁶W. Lambert Gardiner, *Psychology: A Story of a Search* (Belmont, Calif.: Brooks Cole, 1970), p. 11.

⁷John B. Watson, *Behaviorism,* 1st ed. (New York: Norton, 1924) as quoted in James A. Dyal, ed., *Readings in Psychology: Understanding Human Behavior,* 2nd ed. (New York: McGraw, 1967), p. 8.

⁸William James, *The Varieties of Religious Experience* (1902; reprint ed., New York: Mentor, 1958).

⁹Carl Jung, "Synchronicity: An Acausal Connecting Principle," in Robert E. Ornstein, ed., *The Nature of Human Consciousness* (San Francisco: Freeman, 1973), pp. 445-57.

NOTES

[1] Robert W. Doty, "Philosophy and the Brain," *Perspectives in Biology and Medicine,* vol. 9, no. 1 (1965): 23-35, also found in Francis Leukel, ed., *Issues in Physiological Psychology* (St. Louis: Mosby, 1974), pp. 17-18.

[2] B. F. Skinner, *Beyond Freedom and Dignity* (New York: Bantam, 1972), p. 189.

[3] Ibid., p. 190.

[4] Ibid., pp. 191,193,196.

[5] Desmond Morris, *The Naked Ape* (New York: Dell, 1967), p. 9.

[6] Eugene Linden, *Apes, Men, and Language* (New York: Penguin, 1974), p. 217.

[7] David Barash, *Sociobiology and Behavior* (New York: Elsevier-North Holland, 1977), p. 2.

[8] José M. R. Delgado, *Physical Control of the Mind: Toward a Psychocivilized Society* (New York: Harper, 1971), p. 135.

[9] Konrad Lorenz, *On Aggression* (New York: Bantam, 1971).

[10] Richard Dawkins, *The Selfish Gene* (New York: Oxford University Press, 1976), p. 2.

[11] Skinner, *Beyond Freedom and Dignity,* pp. 139-40.

[12] Elliot Valenstein, *Brain Control* (New York: Wiley, 1973), p. 266.

[13] Robert Sinsheimer, "Genetic Engineering: The Modification of Man," *Impact of Science on Society,* 20 (1970): 279-291, as quoted in Francis Leukel, ed., *Issues in Physiological Psychology* (St. Louis: Mosby, 1974), p. 34.

[14] Alvin Toffler, *Future Shock* (New York: Bantam, 1972); Anthony Burgess, *A Clockwork Orange* (New York: Ballantine, 1972); Aldous Huxley, *Brave New World* (New

NOTES

152

York: Harper, 1969); Albert Rosenfeld, *The Second Genesis* (New York: Random, 1975).

[15] B. F. Skinner, *Walden II* (New York: Macmillan, 1962).

[16] Skinner, *Beyond Freedom and Dignity,* pp. 204-5.

[1] Mark P. Cosgrove, *The Essence of Human Nature* (Grand Rapids: Zondervan, 1977).

[2] Jose M. R. Delgado, *Physical Control of the Mind: Toward a Psychocivilized Society* (New York: Harper, 1971), p. 108.

[3] Valenstein, *Brain Control,* p. 87.

[4] Delgado, *Physical Control of the Mind,* p. 108.

[5] Wilder Penfield, as quoted in John Eccles, "Brain and Free Will" in Globus et al., eds., *Consciousness and the Brain* (New York: Plenum, 1976), p. 118.

[6] John Eccles, "How Dogmatic Can Materialism Be?" in Globus et al., eds., *Consciousness and the Brain* (New York: Plenum, 1976), p. 158.

[7] Delgado, *Physical Control of the Mind,* p. 114.

[8] Ibid., pp. 144-45.

[9] Ibid., p. 149.

[10] Dennis Coon, *Introduction to Psychology* (St. Paul: West, 1977), pp. 76-77.

[11] Neil R. Carlson, *Physiology of Behavior* (Boston: Allyn and Bacon, 1977), p. 7.

[12] Eccles, "Brain and Free Will," p. 113.

[13] Roger Sperry, "Mental Phenomena as Causal Determinants in Brain Function," in Globus et al., eds., *Consciousness and the Brain,* pp. 171-72.

[14] Sperry, "Mental Phenomena," p. 173.

5

[1] A. Sutich, "American Association for Humanistic Psy-

chology: Progress Report." Palo Alto, Calif., Nov. 1, 1962, mimeographed. Quoted in J. F. T. Bugental, "The Third Force," *Journal of Humanistic Psychology*, vol. 4, no. 1 (1964): 22.

[2] Carl Rogers, "Some Issues Which Concern Me," *Journal of Humanistic Psychology*, vol. 12, no. 2 (1972): 45-60.

[3] Carl Rogers, "Toward a Science of the Person," *Journal of Humanistic Psychology*, vol. 3, no. 2 (1963): 89.

[4] Ibid., pp. 73-74.

[5] J. F. T. Bugental, "The Third Force in Psychology," *Journal of Humanistic Psychology*, vol. 4, no. 1:25.

[6] Ibid., p. 23.

[7] Ibid., p. 24.

[8] Abraham Maslow, "Eupsychia—The Good Society," *Journal of Humanistic Psychology*, vol. 1, no. 2 (1961): 7-8.

[9] Frank Goble, *The Third Force* (New York: Pocket Books, 1971), p. 55.

[10] Ibid., pp. 61-62.

[11] Ibid., p. 115.

E

[1] Francis Schaeffer, *The God Who Is There* (Downers Grove: InterVarsity, 1968), p. 123.

[2] Arthur Custance, *Man in Adam and in Christ* (Grand Rapids: Zondervan, 1975), p. 31.

[3] Frank Goble, *The Third Force* (New York: Pocket Books, 1971), p. 24.

[4] Leon Festinger, *A Theory of Cognitive Dissonance* (Evanston, Ill.: Row and Petersen, 1957).

[5] Victor Frankl, from an address before the Third Annual Meeting of the Academy of Religion and Mental Health, 1962; found in Frank Severin, ed., *Discovering Man in Psychology* (New York: McGraw, 1973), pp. 132-33.

[6] Mark P. Cosgrove and James D. Mallory, Jr., *Mental*

Health: A Christian Approach (Grand Rapids: Zondervan, 1977); Lawrence J. Crabb, *Basic Principles of Biblical Counseling* (Grand Rapids: Zondervan, 1975).

[7] Gary Collins, *The Rebuilding of Psychology* (Wheaton, Ill.: Tyndale, 1977), p. 67.

[8] C. H. Patterson, "Rational-emotive Psychotherapy: Ellis," *Theories of Counseling and Psychotherapy*, 2nd ed. (New York: Harper, 1973), pp. 49-76.

ʒ

[1] For a readable summary of the differences between transpersonal and naturalistic psychologies see Sam Keen, "The Cosmic Versus the Rational," *Psychology Today*, July 1974, p. 59.

[2] *The Journal of Transpersonal Psychology*, vol. 1, no. 1 (1969): i.

[3] Abraham Maslow, "The Farther Reaches of Human Nature," *The Journal of Transpersonal Psychology*, vol. 1, no. 1 (1969): 5-6.

[4] Anthony J. Sutich, "Transpersonal Psychology: An Emerging Force," *Journal of Humanistic Psychology*, vol. 8, no. 1 (1968): 77. Haridas Chaudhuri, "Psychology: Humanistic and Transpersonal," *Journal of Humanistic Psychology*, vol. 15, no. 1 (1975): 7-15.

[5] R. D. Laing, *The Politics of Experience* (New York: Ballantine, 1967).

[6] Keen, "Cosmic Versus Rational," p. 56.

[7] Robert E. Ornstein, *The Psychology of Consciousness*, 2nd ed. (New York: Harcourt Brace Jovanovich, 1977), p. 10.

[8] Arthur Koestler, *The Roots of Coincidence* (New York: Random, 1972).

[9] Arthur Koestler, "Echoes of the Mind," *Esquire*, August 1972, p. 158.

[10] Charles Tart, *Transpersonal Psychologies* (New York: Harper, 1975), p. 5.

[11] Ibid., pp. 20-21.

[12] Ornstein, *Psychology of Consciousness*, p. vii.

[13] J. Y. Lettvin, H. R. Maturana, W. S. McCulloch, and W. H. Pitts, "What the Frog's Eye Tells the Frog's Brain," *Proc. Inst. Radio Engineers*, 47 (1959): 1941-51.

[14] See Ornstein's *Psychology of Consciousness*. This is the main point of his book.

[15] John Lilly and Joseph Hart, "The Arica Training," in Charles Tart, ed., *Transpersonal Psychologies* (New York: Harper, 1975), pp. 329-51.

[16] James Fosshage and Paul Olsen, eds., *Healing: Implications for Psychotherapy* (New York: Human Sciences Press, 1978). R. D. Laing, *The Politics of Experience* (New York: Ballantine Books, 1967). Alan W. Watts, *Psychotherapy East and West* (New York: Ballantine Books, 1961).

[17] Kenneth Ring, "A Transpersonal View of Consciousness: A Mapping of Farther Regions of Inner Space," *Journal of Transpersonal Psychology*, vol. 6, no. 2 (1974): 125-55.

[18] Raymond A. Moody, *Life After Life* (New York: Bantam, 1976).

8

[1] Francis Schaeffer, *The God Who Is There* (Downers Grove, Ill.: InterVarsity, 1968), p. 28.

[2] James Sire, *The Universe Next Door* (Downers Grove, Ill.: InterVarsity, 1976), p. 203.

[3] Rog Phillips, "The Yellow Pill," in *Introductory Psychology Through Science Fiction*, 2nd ed. (Chicago: Rand McNally, 1977), pp. 517-30.

[4] Carlos Castaneda, *A Separate Reality* (New York: Pocket Books, 1973); idem, *Journey to Ixtlan* (New York: Pocket Books, 1975).

[5] Raymond A. Moody, *Life After Life* (New York: Bantam, 1976).

[6] J. Stafford Wright, *Mind, Man and the Spirits* (Grand Rapids: Zondervan, 1973).

[7] Pierre Teilhard de Chardin, *The Phenomenon of Man* (New York: Harper, 1961), p. 11.

[8] Robert W. Doty, "Philosophy and the Brain," *Perspectives in Biology and Medicine* 9 (1), 1965, pp. 23-35, also found in Francis Leukel, ed., *Issues in Physiological Psychology* (St. Louis: Mosby, 1974), pp. 13-20.

[9] Lawrence LeShan, "Physicists and Mystics: Similarities in World View," *Journal of Transpersonal Psychology*, vol. 1, no. 2 (1969): 1-20.

[10] Keen, "The Cosmic Versus the Rational," *Psychology Today*, July 1974, p. 56.

[11] Harvey Cox, "Why Young Americans Are Buying Oriental Religions," *Psychology Today*, July 1977, p. 40.

[12] For a discussion of these, see Nathaniel Lande's *Mindstyles, Life-styles* (Los Angeles: Price, Stern, Sloan, 1976).

[13] Perry London, "The Psychotherapy Boom: From the Long Couch for the Sick to the Push Button for the Bored," *Psychology Today*, June 1974, pp. 63-68.

9

[1] Francis Schaeffer, *The God Who Is There* (Downers Grove, Ill.: InterVarsity, 1968).

[2] Carl Rogers, "Some Questions and Challenges Facing A Humanistic Psychology," *Journal of Humanistic Psychology*, vol. 5, no. 1 (1965): 2.

10

[1] Josh McDowell, *Evidence That Demands a Verdict* (San Bernardino, Calif.: Campus Crusade for Christ, 1972); Clark Pinnock, *Set Forth Your Case* (Chicago: Moody, 1971); Bernard Ramm, *Protestant Christian*

Evidences (Chicago: Moody, 1953); Clifford Wilson, *Rocks, Relics, and Biblical Reliability* (Grand Rapids: Zondervan, 1977).

[2] Bill Gothard, *Character Sketches* (Chicago: Rand McNally, 1976).

NOTES

Altered consciousness:
110-17; as truth, 110-
11; vs. conscious experi-
ence, 111-15
Aquinas, Thomas, 21
Aristotle, 20-21
Attention, and neuron
firing, 55

Behaviorism: 29-31, 40;
operational definitions
in, 31
Behavior modification,
48-49
Bioengineering, 47
Biofeedback, 101-102
Brain: activity of, 55-57;
stimulation of, 57-58.
See also Mind; Split-
brain studies

Cartesian dualism, 23
Christian psychology. See
Christian theism
Christian theism: defini-
tion of, 11; epistemology
of, 136-37; new birth in,
142; and psychology,
143-49
Clairvoyance, 105
Cognitive dissonance, theory of, 84
Conditioning, in behav-
iorism, 44

Consciousness, vs. self-
consciousness, 63-64.
See also Altered con-
sciousness
Counseling techniques, in
humanistic psychology,
77

Darwin, Charles, 27
Descartes, René, 23
Determinism, in natural-
istic psychology, 39-40,
66
Drugs. See Hallucino-
genic drugs
Drug therapy, in natu-
ralistic psychology, 46,
47
Dualism: Greek, 20-21;
problems of, 24. See
also Cartesian dualism;
Parallelism

Eastern religions. See
Transpersonal psychol-
ogy
Electroshock   therapy
(EST), 46-47
Empiricism, a root of psy-
chology, 24-26
Epiphenomenalism, defi-
nition of, 39-40
Epistemology, 13
Esalen Institute, 94

Eupsychia, in transpersonal psychology, 77
Evolution, theory of, 26-28; in naturalistic psychology, 40-41
Extrasensory perception (ESP), 92

Feelings, emphasis on, in humanistic psychology, 89

Gestalt therapy, 94

Hallucinogenic drugs, 100-101; effects of, 104. See also LSD; Mescaline
Human beings: essence of, 14-15; origin of, 15; problems of, 15-16; purpose of, 15
Humanism, 21-22
Humanistic psychology: definition of, 9; epistemology of, 71-73, 87-90; proponents of, 70; and transpersonal psychology, 103-104, 107
Hypnogogic state, 97
Hypnosis, 92

Introspection, in psychophysics, 29

Leibniz, Gottfried, 23
Locke, John, 24
LSD (lysergic acid diethylamide), 101

Materialism, in naturalistic psychology, 52-53, 66
Meditation, 101; effects of, 104
Mescaline, 101
Mind: source of, 66; as tabula rasa, 24; vs. brain, 52-53, 65-67. See also Epiphenomenalism
Monism, 139; Hebraic, 139; materialistic, 28, 139; pantheistic, 129. See also Panpsychism
Mysticism: in Christianity, 116-17; experience of, 104; explanations of, 104-105

Naturalism, and naturalistic psychology, 36
Naturalistic psychology: definition of, 9; epistemology of, 37; and transpersonal psychology, 103-104, 107
Needs, hierarchy of, in Maslow, 85
Neuron firing, 53-55

Out-of-body travel, 106-107

Panpsychism, 129
Parallelism, a type of dualism, 23
Parapsychology, 105-106
Particle physics, 117-19
Plato, 20
Precognition, 105

Psi particles, 106
Psychology: basic assumptions of, 10; fourth force in, 93; roots of, 23-28. *See also* Third Force psychology
Psychophysics, 29
Psychosurgery, 46

Rationalization, 84-85
Reductionism, in naturalistic psychology, 38

Science, rise of, 22-23
Self-actualization, in humanistic psychology, 75, 83-84
Self-consciousness. *See* Consciousness.
Sociobiology, 41
Split-brain studies, 61-65
Structural Integration, 94
Sufism, 94

Teilhard de Chardin, Pierre, 118
Telekinesis, 105
Telepathy, 105
Third Force psychology, 70
Transpersonal psychology: definition of, 9-10; and Eastern religions, 33-34, 121-22; epistemology of, 96-97, 111-12; subject matter in, 92. *See also* Altered consciousness; Mysticism; Panpsychism

Watson, John, 30
World views, psychological: 8-12, components of, 12-17; definition of, 8, 126; effects of, 9; and ethics, 133-34; functions of, 10; importance of, 11-12
Wundt, William, 20, 28-29

Zen, 94